But I'm not a Bad Person

By Lauren M. Traer, RRT

ISBN: 0-9678532-0-6
Copyright © 2000 Lauren Traer
First Printing 2000
Printed in the United States of America
Published by:
Fulfillment Publishing House
% Maggiano & Associates, Inc.
8695 College Parkway
Fort Myers, Florida 33919
Cover Design: Eric Riemenschneider

All rights reserved. No part of this book may be reproduced or transmitted in any form or by any means, electronic or mechanical, including photocopying, recording or by any information storage and retrieval system without written permission from the author, except for the inclusion of brief quotations in a review.

I dedicate this book to the Lord, who has saved me both physically and spiritually. Also, to Jim, Cindy, and Mom and Dad. You have loved me no matter what, and have endured the pain of watching as anorexia and bulimia devoured me.

ACKNOWLEDGEMENTS

I would like to thank some people who have been influential in my life. I would like to thank Pastor Tony Cubello and his family. Tony is the one who finally led me back to the Lord completely. I gave my life to Christ through Tony. God bless you, Tony, and our church, Branch of Life Christian Fellowship. I would also like to thank Dr. Robert Maggiano, his assistant Mickey, Julie, Dee, and all the staff at Associates in Family Medicine. Dr. M. never gave me false hope. He was not afraid to tell me things the way they were and to tell me when I was out of line. He did not mislead me and was always supportive. I thank our friend, Paul, for how kind and caring he has been. I also thank my dear friend Lynda for her compassion, understanding, and acceptance of me. She taught me that it is okay to know my own limitations, and how to say no and not feel guilty for doing so. I thank my childhood friend, Barb, for always supporting me. I love you and your family dearly. I thank my co-workers at Southwest Florida Regional Medical Center for becoming my friends. You welcomed me into the Respiratory Care Department and patiently re-trained me.

I am also thankful for my dog, Indy, who loves me unconditionally. May I learn to love myself and all people that way. Thanks to my friends at Rehabilitation & Healthcare Center of Cape Coral—I miss and love you. I thank Lois Link who I think of as my second mother and Professor Mark Ehman for helping me edit my manuscript. I thank Phyllis Green for her incredible computer skills. I owe her new bifocals.

I thank my brother-in-law and sister-in-law, Cliff and Darlene, for loving me and accepting me into the family with open arms. I thank my sister for her love and encouragement, and for the close bond we now share. I love you with all my heart, Cindy. I thank my parents too, who brought me up in a loving Christian home, where I was not afraid, but was accepted and comfortable. I am so sorry for all the pain this illness has brought on you both.

Especially, I thank Jim. Only you and I know the whole story, and have walked the walk. I love you now and always will. Thank you for not giving up on me, even when I gave up on myself.

Lauren Traer

TABLE OF CONTENTS

FOREWORD iv

1 THE FIRST SIGN OF THYROID DISEASE 1

2 LOVING MEMORIES OF MY CHILDHOOD 1

3 MISDIAGNOSIS AND SEVERE SYMPTOMS 4

4 DIAGNOSIS AND TREATMENT OF GRAVES' DISEASE 7

5 LOOKING FOR LOVE AND ACCEPTANCE 9

6 DISCOVERING ANOREXIA 11

7 MY FIRST HOSPITALIZATION 13

8 MY FIRST BREAKTHROUGH 15

9 MATURING 17

10 DATE RAPE AND SELF-PUNISHMENT 25

11 OUT ON MY OWN 28

12 LIFE-CHANGING DECISIONS 34

13 INTRODUCTION TO PROZAC 38

14 RELAPSING DURING THE HOLIDAYS 40

15 FALLING IN LOVE WITH JIM 43

16 RELAPSING AND LYING 47

17 COMBINING MARRIAGE AND AN EATING DISORDER 50

18	MY SECOND HOSPITALIZATION	57
19	SEARCHING FOR ANSWERS	62
20	LOSING MY LAST OUNCE OF DIGNITY	63
21	DOMESTIC VIOLENCE	67
22	MY MOST CRITICAL RELAPSE	78
23	FEELING LIKE JOB	85
24	SPIRITUAL HEALING AND PROGRESS	88
25	HOW ANOREXIA AND BULIMIA DESTROY THE BODY	99

EPILOGUE	112
GLOSSARY	116
MEDICAL CONSEQUENCES	120
BIBLIOGRAPHY	122
TESTIMONIALS	123

FOREWARD

I met Lauren in 1990, just after she moved to Florida from her home in Ohio. She was 24 years of age, and despite the fact that she was a little on the thin side, she seemed to be a normal, healthy woman. Little did I know what she had been through, or what she and I would eventually experience together.

We had been friends for a few years before we began dating. Later, we were engaged and eventually married. During our dating I began to learn of Lauren's thyroid disease and her eating disorder. We have a little joke between us that the first question I should have asked her was: *"Do you have any medical problems?"* I do not know if that would have changed anything between us, but had I known of her condition, it would have prepared me.

As I learned more about Lauren's illnesses, I realized I could do nothing to help her with her thyroid; but I thought I could help stop her anorexia and bulimia. I had quit smoking and drinking with little difficulty, and I thought I could apply my *"just do it"* philosophy to help Lauren; but this did not work. Each time I found another way to help her, it seemed to fail. This would increase my frustration, anger, and feelings of helplessness towards this disease. I began to think maybe there was nothing I could do to help her; but I refused to stop trying. Sometimes, I think I tried too hard to control what she was doing, and this just seemed to make the problem worse. Through all of this, I have learned more of what "not" to do than what to do. I wanted her to get well. It did not seem much to ask, but I realize now this is a hard disease to fight.

I knew that Lauren could die from this illness, and I always found it hard to prepare myself for that situation. She would always somehow pull through her relapses even though it took longer each time to recover.

We have our good times and our bad times, but with this illness there seems to be more bad times. I never gave up on Lauren even when, at times, things seemed hopeless. One can never give up hoping and trying. I needed

Lauren's help to get through her relapses just as much as she needed mine. Helping her fight this illness was, and still is physically and mentally draining.

My whole life started revolving around her anorexia. When she was doing well, I was doing well. When she would relapse, I would also relapse. Though I never thought of leaving Lauren, I would experience the mental torture of the reoccurrence of this disease.

We have been married for almost four years, and Lauren is once again in recovery and is doing well. My knowledge of her illness has greatly increased over the past two and a half years, but I have yet to understand it entirely.

Both of us have had to endure so much pain as a result of her illness, yet it has brought us closer. We are now more dependent on each other. This, in turn, has made our marriage stronger. I cannot say that dealing with her disease has been enjoyable, but I am glad that I was able to support Lauren so she would not have to go through it alone. This has been very hard on both of us, but I would not trade the knowledge I now have of this illness for the world.

James L. Traer

CHAPTER 1

THE FIRST SIGN OF THYROID DISEASE

"Mommy, where are you? I need you. Please come here, Mommy. They're staring at me. I'm scared that they will hurt me."

It was impossible to escape the cold, hard look in their eyes. I hid behind the drapes in my bedroom window and curled myself up as tightly as I could. The room was very dark and quiet, yet they could still see me and hear me breathe. I held my breath and remained very still. Why were they pursuing me? What had I done that was so bad? I remember my bedroom door opening and the sound of my mother's footsteps. *"Lauren, where are you? Mommy's here now. I can't see you, honey. Let me turn the light on."*

"No, Mommy, don't turn the light on. They will see me and will hurt me. They will point their fingers at me, make fun of me, and laugh at me. They hate me and tell me I am bad. Mommy, am I bad?"

The next thing I remembered was my mother sitting next to me on my bed with her arms wrapped around me. I cried until the tears no longer welled up in my eyes. Mom held me closely to her, stroking my hair with her loving hand. Neither of us realized the magnitude and gravity of what had just taken place. Unbeknown to us, this was one of the first warning signs that I was developing a serious medical problem. My thyroid disease had begun.

CHAPTER 2

LOVING MEMORIES OF MY CHILDHOOD

It is sometimes thought that sufferers of psychological problems/mental illnesses have endured unhappy, abuse-filled childhoods. Nothing could be further from the truth for me.

I had a happy and enjoyable childhood in Ohio. We did

not have much money, and my dad was a job shopper. He never stayed at one place long enough to get a pension. Dad would often quit a job because of a disagreement with a co-worker. However, he always provided for us, and secured another job, using all of his connections as a draftsman. He learned his trade at night school. My mother is my father's second wife. His first marriage produced three daughters, and lasted ten years. The divorce left my father with emotional wounds that took years to heal. My father, who has mellowed quite a bit over the years, reminds me a lot of my husband now. I say this lovingly: My father had a volatile temper when we were small children. We received our share of spankings, and he raised his voice to us frequently, but we were never afraid for our lives. My father was a good provider and a faithful husband. He worked diligently, sometimes at two or three jobs, to make it possible for my mother to stay home at least part-time until my sister and I were a little older.

My parents have always been older than my friends parents, and I am embarrassed to say that when I was younger, this bothered me. I wondered, "Why are mom and dad older? Why can't they be young like so-and-so's parents? They are so old-fashioned." I remember getting teased about the age of my parents, but these comments were not cruel enough to hurt me.

My parents gave my older sister, Cindy, and me the most love, encouragement, and support that they could give. They made sure that we were treated equally. My mother did not get married until she was 35 years old. Indeed, she had almost given up hope of getting married. Then my father came along. They met at a YMCA activity, and dad had a cast on his foot. His foot had been broken during a skiing accident and mom always said that he could not get away from her fast enough on crutches. It was a difficult time for them financially, since they were paying child support for Dad's first three daughters. Mom made it very clear that she wanted children of their own. My mother is a brilliant woman. She graduated third in her high school class, and could have enrolled in the college of her choice. She was a hard worker and took care of her parents until they passed away. She wanted children so desperately and experienced three miscarriages. Nevertheless, she was determined to have a family of her own, and decided to see a new doctor to aid in this process. My parents diligently and patiently endured many laboratory and diagnostic tests. The results of a standard blood test performed on my mother revealed an abnormality with her thyroid gland, located at the base of the neck. My mother does not recall experiencing any symptoms of thyroid disease, and was surprised by the test results. The physician informed her that her thyroid gland was producing too many antibodies. He prescribed Synthroid, a thyroid hormone that is given orally to regulate thyroid function. My mother became pregnant with my sister shortly after starting on Synthroid. She was very ill when she was pregnant with Cindy and me, yet we were delivered as full-term healthy babies.

Although our family was not financially able to travel much, we were able to take little weekend trips here and there. How my parents afforded to do everything that they did for us is beyond me. There were times when we needed food stamps, and we always had to be very frugal and careful. However, I was able to take singing and dancing lessons for years. Anything we needed, anything we wanted that was in my parents' reach, we were given.

I have many fond memories of my childhood. My mother always made her children her top priority. If we became ill while at school, she was immediately there to take us home and care for us. Once the dreaded visit to the pediatrician was over, we would stop at the pharmacy to buy our medicine. Mom allowed us to pick out one toy that we could hold and play with during our recuperation.

Mothers are very clever. We were persuaded to take our medicine through use of the "medicine seat." This was simply the step leading from our kitchen to our dining room. When we sat on the medicine seat with Mom beside us our fears and apprehensions were relieved. We were safe there on the seat with Mom, because we knew she would never intentionally give us anything that could harm us. How I miss the naivety, security, and blind faith that I had then.

My parents have very high moral values, and they

brought us up with those values. They set an example for us to follow by not drinking, smoking, or taking drugs. My father may have had an occasional cigar when we were toddlers, but not anymore. We attended the United Church of Christ every Sunday as a family, and Cindy and I participated in Sunday School and Youth Group activities. We learned the Golden Rule: "Do unto others as you would have them do unto you." We respected, worshiped, and admired the Lord. We were taught to respect others, especially those in a position of authority. We were told to mind our parents, and to not have sexual relations until we were married. Also, the one thing that having elderly parents did for me was to teach me to respect senior citizens and to be very comfortable around them. Now, in my career as a respiratory therapist, I work specifically with the elderly. I love my patients dearly, and I credit my parents for that.

CHAPTER 3

MISDIAGNOSIS AND SEVERE SYMPTOMS

When did my health problems start? I began developing nervous habits in my younger years. I remember rapidly blinking my eyes, frowning, and making a chewing, twitching motion with my lips. I also twirled my hair repeatedly and talked very fast.

These habits became more pronounced when I was 12 years old and in the sixth grade. I experienced difficulty falling asleep at night. As a result, I was very tired and groggy at school, and found it hard to concentrate on my studies. My mother began to suspect a possible thyroid imbalance in me. She was told that thyroid diseases were usually hereditary, and she had been learning more about the associated symptoms. It was my mother who insisted that the pediatricians check me for thyroid disease. When they finally consented, the laboratory blood test results came back within normal limits. One of the most frustrating aspects about this disease is that the blood tests for it are not conclusive; the results can be negative one time and positive another time. Due to misleading results, it can take years to be accurately diagnosed, as it did for me. I began to think that I was abnormal. Was I imagining the pain and discomfort? Was this what puberty was all about? How could I have these symptoms, yet not have anything wrong with me?

My nervousness and difficulty in falling asleep continued, and I began to withdraw from my family and friends. I became mildly paranoid, and believed that strangers were watching me.

My feelings of abnormalcy gained strength and credibility when the pediatrician referred me to a psychologist. My parents gently and cautiously discussed this issue with me, and asked me if I would go. My mother vividly remembers my reply: *"Please take me to a doctor who can help me."*

I had two sessions with a young female psychologist. She was very nice, but we really did not have much to talk about. I loved my family, was enjoying school, and earning good grades. I remember thinking that I must not be answering correctly, because she kept asking me the same questions over and over. Perhaps she thought I was holding back information out of fear. I may have been uncomfortable during those sessions, but I was always truthful.

My father had lost his job, which temporarily left us without health insurance coverage. My parents were unable to afford my sessions, and were forced to terminate them. I know that they agonized greatly over this decision. We discussed it as a family, and concluded that the sessions did not seem to be helping me.

I slept a little better over the next year or two, and my nervousness decreased. I started high school, and I participated in the marching band, choir, and pom-pom squad. I made many new friends and was a good student academically.

I was 14 years old when the symptoms of my yet-undiagnosed illness recurred and became very severe. I was hyperactive and developed painful, throbbing headaches. It felt like someone was taking concrete blocks and throwing them down on my head. I could hear and feel the pounding in my head. The headaches were so severe that I would try to put my head between my legs to make them go away, getting down on my hands and knees on the floor. Pain relievers brought no relief to me. I would scream and cry and beg for the pain to go away.

My body was constantly working overtime. Everything was going three times faster than it should, and my system simply could not handle it. I developed a higher pain tolerance, and accepted my symptoms as a normal part of life.

I noticed that even though I was very athletic, active in gymnastics and other sports, I would get extremely short of breath during practices, and start sweating at the least exertion. I became unable to walk up a flight of stairs without gasping for breath. I could be sitting in the middle of class in high school and would start perspiring. That became an embarrassment for me. I carried tissues in my purse to blot my face. I prayed that the other students would not notice, or make fun of me. My hair was thinning a little bit, and I was not getting my menstrual periods at all. My eyeballs protruded, which upset me greatly. I felt less and less attractive as the symptoms increased. I was eating large amounts of food eight or nine times a day, and it was never enough to fill or satisfy me. I was a nervous wreck. Due to an increased metabolic rate, my body burned off the extra calories I ate, and I maintained a normal body weight. I am 5'5", and I probably weighed about 115 pounds. I am sure that my overeating affected me psychologically and led to depression. I felt that I could not control my eating habits. People noticed how much I was eating, and made painful remarks to me. This only proved to me that I must not be normal.

CHAPTER 4

DIAGNOSIS AND TREATMENT OF GRAVES' DISEASE

I needed to have a complete physical examination before I could compete on our high school gymnastics team. My mother decided that it was time for a new medical opinion of my condition, and scheduled an appointment for me with her physician. He ordered some standard laboratory blood tests and found that my thyroid levels were three times higher than the normal limit. This meant that my gland was extremely overactive, and I was diagnosed with Graves' disease, also known as Hyperthyroidism. The incidence of Graves' disease is higher in females.

The doctor told us that I had inherited my thyroid abnormalities from my mother. My mother suffered a lot of guilt as a result.

My sister was also tested for thyroid abnormalities and the laboratory results were negative. At first I envied her freedom from this disease, and pouted and complained that it was not fair to me. I am ashamed of how I behaved. I soon became thankful that Cindy was not suffering the way I was.

My parents and I consulted with an endocrinologist, and were presented with three possibilities for thyroid treatment. They were recommended in this order. For the first, I would take the medication Propylthiouracil. Propylthiouracil, also known as PTU, is a thyroid hormone antagonist that inhibits thyroid hormone formation. Upon completion of this treatment, I would take the same medication as my mother, Synthroid, for the rest of my life. The correct dosage would be determined by prescribed blood testing.

The second option was for me to drink radioactive iodine, which destroys thyroid tissue. This procedure would burn away 90 percent of my thyroid gland, after which I would again take Synthroid for the rest of my life.

The last possibility was surgery. An incision would be made all the way across my neck, leaving a large scar. The thyroid gland lies next to the larynx (vocal cords) and

7

calcium gland. We were told that even the most stable-handed surgeon could make a mistake and leave me calcium-dependent for the rest of my life. I could also lose my voice and require a tracheotomy to breathe.

We chose the first option. I remember taking about nine Propylthiouracil pills per day. I had never had any allergies to medicine before this. My reaction to this medicine was swift and severe. My lips swelled up and my forehead jutted out a few inches. Anywhere I scratched, my skin rose, and I itched so horribly that I would immerse myself in cold water, desperate to find relief. I was running high fevers and was very ill. My doctor, wanting to be sure that my reaction was from the medicine and not from a particular food that I had eaten, instructed me to continue taking the medicine. I had the same reactions, but worse. This time, I ended up in the emergency room and was given shots of Benadryl, an anti-inflammatory drug given to reduce swelling. I was overwhelmed by feelings of fear and frustration. I wanted to ask the doctor, *"Why did you let this happen to me again? Do you know how awful I feel, and how much I am suffering? Do you care?"*

I was 14 or 15 years old, in high school, and very self-conscious. Luckily, this reaction happened during spring break from school. I was in tears quite often, and felt frightened and anxious. My mother was present with me throughout all this. No matter how ugly and misshapen I was, she hugged and kissed me. I remember that the doctors instructed me to drink lots of fluids, and I drank them by the gallon. I just wanted this horrible experience to end.

After the failure of this treatment, my parents and I decided to go to the Cleveland Clinic for a second opinion. The endocrinologists were very kind, and ordered thyroid function tests and reuptake scans. Thyroid function tests can reveal evidence of increased or decreased function of the thyroid gland. They include clinical physical examination and reliable laboratory tests. During the reuptake scans, I was exposed to an extremely high level of radium, but was told this was a necessary step in my treatment. I trusted the doctors and wanted to get well. My mom accompanied me to the clinic for each test. My sister was in college and my dad worked, so it was just mother and daughter most of these times. We did not live in Cleveland, and it was almost an hour drive each way. We always had a couple of hours of free time between the uptake scans. Mom and I would walk across the street to the Cleveland Art Museum. In front of the building was a big outdoor pond, and it was such a beautiful time of the year. The springtime temperatures were in the 70's with radiant sunshine. I drank liquid radioactive iodine by sipping it through a straw, and was sent home later that day. I had to be careful not to let people too close to my neck, put their fingers in my mouth, or drink from my glass for about a week. The doctors assured me that I would not glow like an alien. My family was a bit frightened at the treatment and I began to feel isolated, like an outcast distanced from them. After drinking the radioactive iodine, I was told that I must not throw up for a week, or the medicine would not stay in my body and be effective. The doctors were aware of my different eating habits and suspected the development of an eating disorder. They told my mother not to force me to eat during this time. Rather, if I wanted to drink a milkshake, I could have it or whatever else I could allow myself. I remember eating some carrots and cheese, and I think I let myself have a milkshake now and then. I did not throw up the medicine, and was then started on Synthroid, the replacement therapy.

CHAPTER 5

LOOKING FOR LOVE AND ACCEPTANCE

During this time, I was chosen for and enrolled in modeling school. I cannot say that my self-esteem was low at that point, but the anticipation of becoming a model definitely elevated my moods. I remember my father telling me that he did not want me to get a "swelled head". And, I was told by the school that I would be prettier and more successful if I lost five pounds. I guess what I was really looking for, throughout all this, was acceptance. We are brought up in a society that says if you are beautiful, you will be successful. Success, to me, meant being more like my sister. I was very jealous of her. The ironic part, though, was that I was not jealous because of beauty (not that my sister is not an attractive woman), but rather, I was envious that she was four years older. She got to do things first, she did not have Graves' disease, and, most importantly, she had a relationship with my father that I felt I did not have. We both exhibited typical teenage rebelliousness, but I felt that she always knew exactly how to talk to my father and please him, something I could not do. I think that I was trying to be the "beautiful one," and I wanted to impress both my father and other people. Mostly, though, I wanted people to like me. Then, maybe, I would like myself.

Being a teenager and trying to figure out how to look physically is difficult. I have one picture of myself in my pom-pom uniform, which hangs on my refrigerator. It was taken between six months and a year before all the rules and restrictions of anorexia and debilitating symptoms of thyroid disease began to affect me. I was free then. I cannot remember how it feels to be able to eat without restrictions, to feel good about myself, or to look at food comfortably.

I think back to those times, and the scary part is that the more weight I lost, the more distorted my body image became. I did think that I became more attractive as I lost weight. I cannot say that I ever felt fat. A common misconception about this disease is that young women who are suffering from it perceive themselves to be fat. However, I think that what young women desperately want is attention, love, and self respect. What they end up with is a horrible, life-altering illness that cannot be controlled. For some, it can be merely a "teenage disease". If therapy and medication are administered at the onset, it can be conquered before the scars are too deep. But, for those of us who are chronically anorexic/bulimic, I do not think it will ever end. And the scars, both physical and mental, are permanent.

CHAPTER 6

DISCOVERING ANOREXIA

Anorexia started rather easily. I remember watching a television movie about a young woman who was anorexic. One of the ways she lost weight was by forcing herself to vomit after she ate. She did this by sticking her fingers down her throat, causing herself to gag. I was fascinated, and felt like I had just stumbled upon this wonderful secret. It sounded easy enough, and I was anxious to try it myself. One night after dinner, I excused myself and headed straight for the bathroom. I locked the door and knelt down in front of the toilet. I stuck two fingers down my throat and started to gag, yet nothing came up. My eyes watered and my nose ran, but I could not vomit. After numerous times, I finally succeeded in bringing some food up. I was out of breath, exhausted, and frustrated. There had to be an easier way to throw up! I soon discovered that by pushing inward and upward on my stomach, an inch above my navel, I could easily force myself to vomit. I quickly learned what foods were easy to throw up. During the very first phases of experimentation, I do not believe that my actions could be considered a disease. I was exploring the act of having control over my body. I took pride in my first five pound weight loss, and started to like and approve of myself. I was proud of myself because I had done something successfully. Unfortunately, I was unable to allow myself to eat enough to maintain my weight, and dropped to about 90 pounds. The more weight I lost, the prouder I was of myself, and the more I liked myself.

The anorexia continued to blossom and develop. When my disease became common knowledge, I had just completed my thyroid treatment. Doctors believed that if the thyroid problems were stabilized, the anorexia would also cease. Thyroid imbalances have been proven to cause mental disorders on their own. My parents clung desperately to that theory, but their hopes were soon shattered. This was the first of a long line of disappointments that we would experience.

I began losing a few more pounds, cutting back on what I ate, and practicing how to make myself throw up. I developed a large bruise from pushing on my stomach so frequently. It became very painful. I ate ice cream because I could regurgitate it easily. I think that I was mentally ready to stop losing weight after the first ten pounds, but since I was unable to allow myself to eat enough food to maintain that weight, I continued downward. I am thankful that I did not abuse diet pills to lose weight. I sporadically took laxatives, knowing that diarrhea would make my stomach flatter.

I remember stealing diuretic pills from my parents' medicine cabinet. They had been prescribed for our family dog, and I swallowed half of the bottle. Needless to say, I spent the remainder of the day in the bathroom! But, the more fluid I lost, the flatter my stomach became, and the happier I was.

I do not know the precise cause of my anorexic behavior. I cannot pinpoint anything, although I do believe that my participation in modeling school was a contributing factor. I began to idolize thin, bony women. I remember a girl at my high school who was extremely thin. Her clothes hung on her, and I thought that she looked wonderful. I wanted to look like her.

I was also influenced during my gymnastics training. When I was about 10 years old, I decided that I wanted to be a gymnast. I was exposed to the sport through gym class at my school. A few of my female classmates had been training for years and were very good gymnasts. I admired how firm, thin, and muscular their bodies were. I scrutinized my own body, and was dissatisfied with my appearance. I wanted to be as graceful and talented as they were.

My parents gave permission for me to enroll in gymnastics lessons. Most of the girls in my age group had been training since they were little girls, and were at a more advanced level than me. I was placed in the beginner's class. I was the oldest and biggest girl in the class, and quickly became self-conscious and uncomfortable. This only grew worse as I entered puberty and began to mature. I did not want breasts and curves. I wanted to have a little girl's body. I wanted to be as tiny as the other gymnasts.

My skills as a gymnast improved, but I always felt inferior to my teammates. I felt large and awkward.

CHAPTER 7

MY FIRST HOSPITALIZATION

As recourse for starving myself, I was admitted to a children's hospital psychiatric ward at the age of 15. I was given liquid supplements and told that I needed to start eating. I cannot blame anyone who treated me this way, because that was all that was known at the time. And, some action had to be taken. I learned that if I could eat a lunch and dinner in the same day, I would be released sooner. The patients in the ward went out on group trips to the park and bowling alley. We all started at the bottom, Level 1. As I advanced to the next level, I was given more freedom and could walk around the rest of the hospital by myself for an hour at a time. I really enjoyed that time. A couple of my girlfriends and my minister came to see me. They were noticeably uncomfortable around me, and I cried bitterly after they left. The doors to the outside were locked and I was left to suffer alone in my room that night.

I gradually started eating. I had a sandwich for lunch, and a sandwich and maybe something else for dinner. Gradually, I added a few more foods, because I knew that this was my guarantee of release. I had to face and fight the "beast" each time I tried to progress and eat more. No matter what I did or where I went, it was in me, destroying me.

The first time I saw a patient placed in restraints, I was very upset. I felt very uncomfortable, and was scared that I too might be locked in the quiet room if I misbehaved. A lot of yelling, screaming, and crying took place daily in the ward. I was the only anorexic in the locked unit, and I just wanted to go home. I begged them to let me go home. But my sobs and requests fell on deaf ears.

No one paid attention to my feelings. The three of us went to family therapy—my father, my mother, and myself—my sister was away at college. We all tried to do what we were told, and I finally gained enough weight to be released from the psychiatric ward. I wanted to start my junior year in high school and had probably gained about five pounds. I returned to school as an emaciated replica of what I once was. I was so cold that I wore sweaters in the summer. The little hairs on my arms stood up on end, and I always had goose bumps. I dealt with many questions when I went back. I had been fairly popular, but rumors were circulating that I had this disease, this anorexia. I was uncomfortable at school, and the tension was hard on my friends. I isolated myself, because I did not understand the disease enough to help them understand it. I felt like the only one who had these awful, dark feelings, the only one who wanted to harm herself. I began to believe that I was a bad person, and must have done something horrible to be given this disease. My friends did not know what to say to me. They simply perceived my growing isolation and increased depression as separation from them. I loved my friends. I wanted to do things with them, but it was all I could do to stay alive.

I lost the five pounds I had gained prior to leaving the hospital, and continued sessions with the psychiatrist as an outpatient. When my weight continued to plummet, the doctor wanted to hospitalize me again. I begged, pleaded, screamed, and cried because I believed with all my heart that the psychiatric ward was the wrong place for me. It was not going to help me and would not be what I needed. I did not know what I needed, but I resisted returning to the locked unit. I had flashbacks of the nights I cried alone in my room, and the many times security was called to quiet a disruptive patient. My mother supported me, and said that she and my father were going to keep me at home for now. That was an extremely painful and gut-wrenching decision for my parents to make.

Family therapy taught me that my mother was overprotective, my father did not love me enough, and that I was a selfish little brat who only thought of herself. I really believed this, and grew to despise myself more and more. What kind of child was I? How could I do this to my parents? I will never fully let go of the guilt I felt as I watched my mother cry and my father pace the floor. I was supposed to be their pride and joy. If I really loved and respected them, why was I putting them through this? My wonderful parents went to every family therapy meeting. My father walked out of one of them because he got mad, but he came back the next week. We also took part in group therapy in which sufferers and their families could come together for support and understanding. We attended every weekly meeting for about a year. I also had sessions with a guidance counselor at my high school. Unfortunately, the latter only did more damage. Another anorexic girl was with me during these sessions, and we ended up competing with one another to see who could be the skinniest and sickest. The main idea that the guidance counselor wanted to get across was *"think of your mothers, think of how you're breaking their hearts,"* which only gave me another reason to despise myself.

Sadly, this led me to believe that I was an evil, awful daughter. How could I do this to my parents? How could I do this to my mother? I must be punished for this rebellious behavior…

I would then eat and throw up again.

CHAPTER 8

MY FIRST BREAKTHROUGH

My first breakthrough came during practice for the pom-pom squad. I forced myself to continue working out with the team despite my malnourished and weakened condition. I knew I would be unable to quit without feeling like a failure. Somehow, I found the strength to perform with them at our high school basketball games. At that point, my daily intake was one meal, consisting of either celery with peanut butter, or carrots dipped in salad dressing. If I was feeling generous, I added a slice of cheese. I would not let myself eat this until around 6 p.m., due to my very scheduled eating and anorexic rules. I would check my stomach every day, throughout the day, to make sure that it had not grown or protruded outward. This was extremely important to me. During the winter months, I remember sitting practically inside our fireplace at home, with my pajamas on, trying to warm myself. I shivered from the cold temperature and from my fears, despite the warmth of the flames. I did not know how my body looked, yet I did not feel fat.

One day during practice, I turned around in front of the full-length mirrors. For the first time ever, I saw an emaciated woman, and it scared me. I thought, *"I look awful! I want to change!"* That was a monumental step. The next breakthrough came about a month later. The local news had a story on anorexia, and showed a picture of an anorexic girl in her bra and underwear. Once again, the *"I look awful! I want to change!"* reaction took place. I saw her hip bones and ribs sticking out, and I realized that was how I looked. It was time to get the courage to change my eating habits, but I did not know how to do that. I was petrified. How could I like myself and eat more? I was proud of the tight control I had over my food intake. How would I know when to stop eating, and what was a normal portion of food? How would I know what to eat and what not to eat? I had no idea, and felt very lost and alone, like an abandoned child.

When I first gained the weight back, it was very difficult. It was like learning how to eat all over again. Compared to what I go through now, I would say that it was almost easy. Of course, that was not true. Learning how to let my body feel full and to learn when to stop eating meant standing up to the "beast". I believe that is why I became bulimic as well. After starving myself for so long, allowing myself to eat again was frightening and exhilarating. I wanted to eat all the previously forbidden foods. But I did not want to stop eating, because I had been ravenously hungry for so

long. I would then eat too much, feel full and bloated, and make myself throw up. The damage would begin again, and the victory would go to the "beast".
I tried to eat more. The first few times I ate too much, and made myself throw up. That was disappointing and heartbreaking, but I did not give up. I gradually learned to eat some different foods and, actually, I regained most of my weight. I weighed about 105 pounds, and was eating enough to maintain the weight. I did not eat much at lunchtime, maybe a candy bar and an apple, and then I would have a big hamburger or piece of chicken for dinner, followed by some popcorn in the evening. It was not "normal", but it was enough to keep my weight stable.

CHAPTER 9

MATURING

Despite my eating disorder, I matured into a young woman. My eating patterns and schedules placed numerous restrictions on me. I started working at age 16 at, of all places, a Dairy Queen. People used to laugh at the irony of that. Why, a bulimic must be as happy as a pig in mud. Unlimited ice cream and treats were at my fingertips. I was employed there periodically for about four years, and I actually enjoyed it. But my eating problems continued. We were allowed to buy food at a discount, which I did at times, especially when I was in a bulimic relapse. There was only one bathroom in the store, that all of us, including the customers, had to share. There was no guarantee that I would be able to throw up when I needed to. I remember feeling angry, irritated, and panic-stricken if I had overeaten and was unable to sneak away and vomit. *"I can't possibly keep this down—I just ate two large sundaes. Why do customers have to come now? Someone, please, give me a way out—Help Me!"* My co-workers and bosses must have been suspicious, but probably did not form opinions because of lack of information concerning eating disorders. However,

17

I think that working also helped my self-esteem and outlook. I was earning money and accumulating some savings, of which I was proud,
 I financed the bulimia from money I saved from my job. The binges consisted mostly of junk food, such as chips, candy, cookies, and ice cream. These were all items that I would never let myself eat and keep down, food that was taboo until relapse time. Other people could eat whatever they desired, but not me. If I did, I would be an ugly, gigantic pig. How could I live with myself?

I spent the following summer with my sister in Maryland, where I got a job with IBM in the chemical coding lab. She was working for IBM and helped me to get the job. The "new girl at the office" was easily making friends and becoming very popular with the men. I could not believe the attention I was receiving and kept asking myself, *"Is this really happening to me?"* The questions soon became *"Can I handle this? Do I deserve this? What could be so special about me?"* I could not see the Lauren that they saw, and wished to God that I could. I earned enough money that summer to buy a nice car, and felt that my life was improving.

I returned home that fall, decided to change my major course of study in college, and enrolled at the University of Akron. Life was a bit harder in college, especially during my periods of relapses. I would be able to go for days without binging and purging, but always managed to squeeze in the treasured days of self-abuse. I commuted to classes and lived at home with my parents. I binged and purged while they were gone. This is obviously not something one wants to do in front of anyone. I began another stretch of recovery, and ate the most "normally" than I had in a long, long time. I ate lunches and dinners, and in the same day! The anorexia soon reared its ugly head, and I cut down to one meal per day.

 I had a new boyfriend with whom I was very seriously involved. He was the first of many with whom I fell in love. He was wonderful to me and loved me deeply. I was happier than I had been in years.
 I think that without the rituals and bondage from an eat-

ing disorder restricting me, this relationship could have led to marriage. I was too paranoid about my disease to enjoy this happiness. He and I had many good times together, and I refrained from throwing up for nearly a year. However, I was not eating enough. I ate once per day, and only in the evening. Since I was not throwing up, I thought I was doing well and accepted these limitations. I tried to overlook how hungry I was, and the fact that I was depriving myself. My weight was staying on because I had not yet started on my exercise plan.

I did well in the respiratory therapy program at college. I ended up taking a year off to work at a local hospital to make sure that respiratory therapy was the right career for me. The man I was involved with was a student in the program with me. Months later, I began closing the door to my heart, and excluded this man from my life. I was frightened of letting anyone get close to me because of the disease I had. I did not want to lose him—I loved him. But I was abnormal, and felt marked by the "beast". I would only bring him pain and suffering, just as I had to my parents. How could I even think of myself as a wife? How would I explain my bizarre eating schedules? How do I cook for my husband, sit across from him and watch him eat, while I did not? He would try to be patient and help me, but would eventually give up out of frustration. He would find it insulting when I did not eat with him, and would think that I just did not care to do so. He would think I was weird, crazy, and would reject me. But wait a minute…Can I not explain to him that the disease makes me act this way? Can I not make him see that I am good and the disease is bad? No—because I do not believe that myself. Finally, he would leave me, and would see me as a failure who could not take control over her problems. And I would be left alone, to sit in silence with my shame.

After the year off from school, I returned to the respiratory program and graduated with honors. My weight stayed fairly low during that time, at 95-100 pounds, but I kept the throwing up under control. I was able to focus on my studies and lead what I thought was a fairly normal life. The "beast" was still in me, but he had fallen asleep.

The naps never lasted very long, and the relapses always returned. I believe they stemmed from deprivation. When I did eat, it was only vegetables or fruits, and after eating this sparsely for a few months, my body started craving the forbidden foods. Why could other people enjoy what I could not? What was wrong with me?

I never became a smoker or drinker out of the fear of becoming an addict. I knew what it was like to be addicted to something that was so strong, had such control over me, and could ruin my life. As a teenager, I had an occasional drink and tried to smoke a cigarette here and there, but I was too afraid of addiction to continue on that path. All or nothing was the way I looked at everything. I was very obsessive/compulsive, and the medications used today for treatment were not yet available. Obsessive/compulsive disorders were not out in the open or publicized. Obsession/compulsion is an essential part of all addictive diseases. None of us wants to be an addict; none of us chooses that road. I did not wake up one day when I was ten years old and say, okay, "I choose to have an eating disorder." Nor did I want these obsessive/compulsive thoughts to dwell in my mind. I wanted to be in charge of me. I did not want to be a begrudgingly obedient servant to these overpowering thoughts. I just wanted to be like everyone else.

During my last semester of college, I started working at a hospital for infants and children. A girlfriend and co-worker of mine convinced me to join a health club. That seemed to be a cure for a while because I began working out. I was still thin, but I went to the gym every day loyally. It helped me because I realized that I could let myself eat more if I was working out. It was extremely difficult to allow myself to eat more. Eating one extra apple a day is entering the war zone of one's mind. Is it too much? Do I feel too full too early in the day? It is the hardest thing, talking oneself into eating more, yet not feeling like an ugly pig after one does. Very gradually, I increased my food intake. I liked the aerobics classes so much that I became an instructor. My new daily routine became: go to the health club in the morning, work out, take a shower, and go to work. I was transferred from the night shift to the evening shift at the hospital. I looked the healthiest and was eating the best that I had in a while. My weight increased, and I comfortably wore leotards around the gym. Men paid attention to me, and frequently asked me out on dates. The club was like my second home. It was a safe zone for me, in a non-threatening environment. I felt accepted and loved by the members. I felt proud of myself, and I liked the image I saw in the mirrors. That was a dramatic change for me.

The illness and course of treatment, this up and down roller coaster, has been going on ever since. I have been a patient of eight different psychiatrists and have seen each for about a year. It is very disheartening to learn that there is no cure for eating disorders, that they are fatal. They will destroy the mind and body of the sufferer. We are supposed to be optimistic, stay upbeat and keep trying, which is much easier said than done. I also saw an initially encouraging psychologist. He had discovered a new way to treat eating disorders, and I was told that within six months I would never throw up again. At that point I was maintaining a normal body weight, but I was binging and purging in secret. I remember thinking, although I was skeptical, he has got to be kidding! This is incredible! I placed my hopes and dreams on this new therapy, and really believed that this was the cure for which I had been searching. No more suffering and living in fear! I was on my way to freedom. My expectations and hopes were crushed when, after being his patient for over two years, I was far from being cured. The urges to binge and purge never stayed away for very long, and I continued to submit to them after lengthy periods of fighting. I have also tried different medicines. About four or five years ago, medical science announced that some antidepressants had been found to be very helpful with eating disorders. I have had long periods of help from Prozac. It is an anti-depressive and anti-compulsive medicine taken orally. It does seem to help me fight the urges to binge and purge. The very first time I tried Prozac, and it helped my urges, I could have kissed every human being on the face of the earth. I felt confident, stable, and my self-esteem was elevated. I would have given both my arms and legs to feel that way forever, and all I could do was wonder whether this was the way that most people felt. Did they not feel those awful desires to hurt themselves and to be so compulsive? Were they able to accept life and themselves? If so, how?

I cannot say that I have ever been able to eat normally since then. I have had periods during which my weight has been statistically normal for my height. I have had long stretches of "being on the wagon," of not torturing myself through binging and purging. I have been blessed by graduating with honors from college. I may have changed my major a few times, but I eventually made a good career choice. I became a registered respiratory therapist, and I passed my Boards with high scores. I have worked in areas from management to neonatal to subacute care to diagnostic testing. I have really been able to branch out and learn new skills, and I feel very fortunate for these opportunities. I truly enjoy my profession.

I also have had many boyfriends and have dated steadily. However, I allowed the shame I felt inside to break up many relationships. I felt disgusting, filthy, and dirty after vomiting—why would a man want to touch or love me, let alone kiss me? If he knew what I did, he would surely leave me. I have learned that I cannot control the thoughts, urges, and compulsions that enter my head, along with the fears and unsettlings. But what I must do is never to let down my guard. I must never quit fighting the "beast".

I used to think that thyroid disease and an eating disorder were specific curses on me. My friends do not have them, nor does my sister. Why me? People think that I am doing this to myself just for attention. I do not believe that anybody would want an addiction where they sell their soul to feed an addiction, then hate themselves vehemently for doing so. Nobody wants to bear the cross of shame. Imagine trying to explain it to someone: *"Well, I either don't eat, or I eat everything in sight, then throw it up."* The first thing that people say is *"that's disgusting."* It is disgusting and incomprehensible. Why else would sufferers do whatever it took to hide it. I lied to conceal the binging and purging because I was so afraid that my future husband would leave me if he discovered what I was doing. The clandestine binging and purging only left me with frustration and everlasting pain.

I used to ask myself: How can a woman who is intelligent and attractive purposely ruin herself? One answer is that I was not able to handle my own successes and take pride in them. Although I did a little modeling, I never finished modeling school. At that point, I had become very ill with the anorexia and was hospitalized. But, I think that some of what the school taught me stayed with me. The bottom line was: The thinner the better. Thinness equals success. I was never really comfortable with my weight after that, and I just did not know how I looked. The illness was not out of control yet. I was still able to live and deal with it, and have a fairly normal life throughout the end of high school and the beginning of college. Life was a bit harder in college, especially during my periods of relapses. I would be able to go for days without binging and purging, but always managed to squeeze in the treasured days of self-abuse. I lived at home with my parents while I commuted to school, and binged and purged while they were gone. This is obviously not something one wants to do in front of anyone.

The repercussions were severe because I would internalize it, thinking: *"My family hates me, and will be so mad at me when they find out that I've thrown up."* When they became angry, they did not know how to show that anger, and they did not know how to separate me from the illness. The illness is about having no love or respect for oneself, and the deeper one sinks into its dark, lonely pit, the stronger it gets. Consequently, the less respect I had for myself, the more I binged and purged. It became a vicious cycle. Add to that the guilt I felt over what my actions were doing to my family, and the self-beating became more severe. I started to get a sort of comfort from being as weak and crippled as I would become after days of throwing up and starvation. On the day after a relapse, I could allow myself to eat and feel good about it. My stomach was flat and empty, which gave me a sense of security. This was the closest I came to being nice to myself.

My body amazed me. I would have to say that for the

23

first ten years, I was always able to rebound from the relapses. The scar on my stomach from forcing myself to vomit served as a constant reminder, though. My weight did not fall below 88-90 pounds, and my condition had not yet become life threatening. I was more receptive and willing to try new treatments and therapies at that time. I still had hope of finding a cure, the key that would unlock my chains. Hypnosis, biofeedback, medicine—I tried all of them. As I mentioned before, I thought the health club might be my cure. Since I was exercising and burning off calories, I could allow myself to eat a little more. I followed this path for maybe four or five months, but then I relapsed. Move forward and then slip up. One step forward and two steps back. Each time, it became harder to pull myself out of the relapse, which progressively lasted longer and longer. The feelings of disgust and self-loathing grew stronger and more powerful, and it was increasingly difficult to climb out of the hole I had dug for myself. Also, I continued to push myself: *"How much food can I eat? How much can I shove in my mouth at once?"* In a nonsensical way, it was self-abuse and self-pleasure rolled into one. How else could I eat the entire pot of spaghetti, or two boxes of cereal, as fast and sloppily as I wanted? But the price I paid the next day, physically and mentally, was never worth it.

These are some of the "up" periods for which I am very thankful. I am grateful for the periods of time when I was not throwing up or starving quite so badly that it was inhibiting my life. I appreciate the times when I felt halfway decent about myself, and that I was able to attend and graduate from college. I am thankful that I was able to maintain a normal weight and be found desirable by men during those years. I was fortunate enough to date frequently and have many wonderful boyfriends. It had not yet entered my head that I needed to achieve a critically low weight. I believe that bulimia is brought on by the starvation from anorexia. With anorexia, I deprived myself of food for so long that when I did start eating again, I wanted to eat everything. I did not know how to eat, and felt ashamed of that. I desperately wanted to learn to eat. I wanted to sit down with my parents and eat dinner with them. I wanted to eat balanced meals. But I could not allow myself to do so. The best I could do was to eat a tiny lunch and a good-sized dinner. I could not tolerate breakfast, because I thought that the food I ate would cause my stomach to protrude and look large to others too early in the day. I clung to many rituals and regimens, and experienced fear and anxiety when I tried to let them go.

CHAPTER 10

DATE RAPE AND SELF-PUNISHMENT

Despite my popularity with men, I never believed that I was an attractive woman. It was crucial to my self-esteem that the men I met liked me. They did not have to fall in love with me, just like me. I wanted to be the perfect girlfriend, and made a conscious effort to be agreeable, pleasant, and appealing. I felt guilty if I turned down a sexual advance and hurt the man's feelings. What if he did not like me anymore, or said bad things about me? What if he thinks I am mean? And, I was called a bitch and a tease a few times for not consenting to sexual advances. That hurt me very badly.

It took me until about two or three years ago to remember that I had been date raped in college. I used to wonder how people could shut out such a tortured experience. Now I know, because I did. I recall being at college for about two weeks before that horrible night. My roommate and I were freshmen, wide-eyed and naïve. One night we dressed to the nines, and went out to a nightclub where we could dance. We had so much fun, just dancing and mingling. I was approached by an older, very handsome man, and asked to dance. He said he was a pilot, and showered me with compliments. I was overwhelmed by the whole college atmosphere. For the first time in my life, I believed I was beautiful. This man convinced me that my roommate had left the nightclub with his friend. I realized I had no way home, and felt lonely and abandoned. I knew that the buses back to campus stopped running at midnight. It was past midnight, and my dorm was about three miles away. I felt betrayed by my roommate, and was frightened of being alone. When he offered to give me a ride, I said okay, and got into his car.

I think that I was afraid to say "no", because then he might not like me. He told me that we had to stop at his hotel room so that he could get some things, and asked me to come inside. I made the mistake of entering his room and, before I realized it, the door was locked behind me and I was trapped. He forced me down on the bed, climbed on top of me, and began kissing me. He told me he had a gun, and showed it to me. He also told me repeatedly that he could fall in love with me, and that I was beautiful. When he pinned my arms behind my back, fear and anxiety filled my head. I could not believe this could be happening to me. I was a stranger on campus and far away from my dorm. What was I going to do?

He took off some of my clothes, and I was forced to perform sexual acts against my will. The attack did not involve intercourse, but was restrained, forceful, and unconsented touching. I begged him to stop, but he ignored me. I tried to hold back my tears, and to stay strong. I felt violated, and my heart ached for every woman who had endured such a demeaning and cruel experience. He finally started to fall asleep, but still had his arms wrapped tightly around me. I stayed as still as I could until I could hear him snoring. One inch at a time, I moved away from him, rolled out of bed and onto the floor. I gathered my clothes and began to dress, my hands violently shaking as I attempted to fasten my bra. I think he actually heard me leave, but he did not try to stop me. There I was, alone in the city, at 3:00 a.m., with no idea how to get back to the university. I had very little money, was 18 years old, and had been humiliated and hurt. By the grace of God, I walked the three miles back to my dorm and arrived safely. My roommate had been worried sick about me. She asked me why I had left without her and deserted her. I told her what he had said to me, and realized that he had lied. We hugged each other and I sobbed on her shoulder. I felt so angry with myself for allowing it to happen. How could I be so stupid? I felt dirty, awful, and evil, and was unable to talk about what had happened to me. I had disappointed God and myself. I had not slept all night, and wanted to go home for the weekend. I had to punish myself, and knew just how to do it.

I called my mother, and she came and got me. I binged and purged, slept a little, and felt that I was cleansing myself. I was scrubbing that dirty, awful act off of me.

I returned to school as a wiser and more cautious young woman. However, my self-esteem had been damaged, and I began to lose my self-confidence. I was still obsessed with wanting to please everybody, wanting to be the girl that everybody liked. I was always a hard worker. I tried to resume my classes and campus life.

During the semester I developed a serious sinus infection, and spiked a 105-degree fever. I was hospitalized in an isolation room at the campus clinic for two days. My professors had told me that if I missed even one class, my grade would drop a letter grade. I was an extremely driven student, getting A's, and pushing myself to my limits. I could not miss class! I cried when I was not allowed to have my roommate bring my textbooks to the clinic.

I was given antibiotics and forced to sleep on ice packs to bring down the fever. My body started to heal, and I was discharged from the clinic. I returned to my dorm room and classes. Within one week, the infection and 105-degree fever returned with a vengeance. My ears filled with fluid, and I temporarily lost my hearing. I finally agreed to go home with my mother and see our family doctor. I took all my books with me, and tried to keep up with my lessons. My condition slowly improved with another round of antibiotics. I was back at school within a week, but never felt like my old self again. My memory did not seem as clear and sharp, and some of my thoughts were fuzzy. I think that I let the fever go too long.

My weight remained stable at 110-115 pounds during my freshman year at college, despite bulimic relapses. Ironically, many of my college relapses into bulimia occurred

27

when I should have been enjoying my success and life. If I earned A's on my tests, or had a new boyfriend, I could not accept and enjoy it. I did not feel that I deserved to be happy. Instead, I would fall back to anorexia and bulimia, my security blankets. I endured a lengthy, more serious relapse towards the middle of spring semester. I remember spending my food coupons on junk food at the student center. I waited until my roommate was at class, and binged and purged while she was gone. This took careful planning, since our entire hall shared one communal bathroom. I remember that my roommate became very angry with me when she learned of my disgusting secret, and distanced herself from me. We had become very close friends, and I felt hurt and rejected. I did not understand my disease well enough myself to explain it to her. Therefore, she was confused and unable to be sympathetic. I was too afraid of rejection to reach out to her for help. I began to isolate myself, believing that no one would want to be around someone who vomits. I am sure that she felt helpless and frustrated, and rejected by me. Losing her friendship devastated me and only reaffirmed to me that I was a very bad person.

CHAPTER 11

OUT ON MY OWN

As I continued my search for a way to like myself, I directed my efforts toward moving up the career ladder. With new hope in my heart, I diligently read the want-ads for therapists in my medical journals. I focused on positions available in warm, southern states that would provide opportunities for advancement. I eventually chose Florida for the warmth and sunshine. Since my first thyroid treatment, my body was noticeably sensitive to the cold. I chose a position offering advancement to management, one that even gave me a title on my name badge. Now I could be somebody, and surely I would learn to like myself. I hoped that I could leave the disease in Ohio, move far away and be free. I had studied intensely to earn the credentials needed for this supervisory position at a new hospital. I interviewed, got the job, and returned home to pack my suitcases. I piled my textbooks and suitcases into my car, kissed my parents goodbye, and left in search of happiness.

I am amazed that I found the courage to take such action. I had been born and raised in the same small town, and lived with my parents in the same house, all my life. I was leaving the two people who loved me the most, and always took care of me. My parents were loving and supportive, and allowed me to make this decision on my own. They trusted my judgment, and kept any misgivings they may have had at the time to themselves. Years later, I would learn that they actually wanted to keep me safe at home, but had agreed that they would not stand in the way of the success of their children. My sister had already moved away from home upon graduation from college to further her career. My mother has regretfully said to me, *"Maybe I should have stopped you from leaving. Maybe you never would have become this sick. A mother is supposed to protect her child. Did I fail as a mother?"* With tears in my eyes, I hugged my mother tightly, and replied, *"Mom, there was nothing you could have done to prevent this. This disease would have kept growing and progressing despite what you might have done. Please don't blame yourself. You were the best mother I could have asked for. I'm so sorry for bringing you such pain and misery."* To this day, I remain sorry for that.

Relocating to Florida was one of the hardest decisions I have made in my life. Somehow, I shut the door to my own apprehensions and uncertainties about the move by focusing on two things: (1) freeing myself from the claws of the beast, and (2) finding the key to liking myself.

Why was I doing this? How could I think of leaving my family and friends? I was employed as both an aerobics teacher and a respiratory therapist, and enjoyed each one. I had many boyfriends, and felt accepted at the health club where I taught. Why would anyone leave all this behind?

The answer is very simple: To find the cure for my disease. This thought was what I concentrated on as I walked down the ramp to board the plane (my car was being shipped down separately). My parents have always loved taking people to the airport. They arrive very early and wait until they see the plane take off before they head for home. I remember staring out the tiny airplane window and seeing my parents standing side by side at the gate. My father is fairly tall, and has long arms, so his wave is impossible to miss. As two frightened little girls who had somehow become separated from their parents, all my sister and I had to do was look for Daddy's wave, and we could find our way to safety. As the plane rolled away, the last thing I saw through my tear-filled eyes was Daddy's wave.

Upon arriving in Florida, I became overwhelmed by sudden feelings of loneliness and uncertainty. *"What was I doing here all by myself? Had I made the right decision?"* The only person I knew in Florida was my mother's cousin Ruth, who soon became known as "Aunt Ruth". She had severe lung damage due to emphysema, and was dependent on home oxygen and nebulized breathing treatments to survive. The main reason I chose respiratory therapy as my career was to help people like her. She enjoyed telling people that she was the reason I became a respiratory therapist. Aunt Ruth received her oxygen from a medical equipment company, and was very fond of the deliveryman. She informed me that he had just suffered a broken engagement, had bought a house, and was looking for a roommate to help defray his expenses.

We met, and things fell into place as perfectly as a jigsaw puzzle. His name was Jim, and I thought he had sexy eyes and a cute butt. We agreed to become roommates. Although I was out on my own for the first time, I could not take a complete step into independence. I thought that by living with Jim I would be safe and protected in his home. I was attracted to him, and I thought he would be attracted to me. I was used to men wanting to be around me, being impressed by me, and thinking I was pretty. This was the first man who made it very clear to me from the beginning that he wanted no part of a relationship. He had suffered emotional wounds, and was not interested in becoming involved with another woman. I pursued him anyway, voluntarily setting myself up for disappointment and heartache. Within a month or two, my inevitable rejection came, and I moved out of Jim's house and rented my own apartment. I learned quickly that, as an anorexic/bulimic, living alone was a big mistake. I simple could not handle all that freedom. This was the first time the bulimia spun out of control. As I struggled through a typical day at work, I took comfort knowing that when it was over, I could lock myself in my apartment, shut the blinds, and binge and purge. That was my own so-called Happy Hour, even though it brought me no happiness. I may have experienced feelings of relief and freedom, but certainly not happiness. The last hour in the workday seemed to last forever, and I practically raced out the doors to my car. I drove directly to the grocery store, hoping that the checkout lines would not be too long, and that I would not run into anyone I knew. How could I possibly explain a whole cart full of groceries, when everyone knew I was single and living alone? This was the only time in my life that I permitted myself to spend money freely. I still tried to buy sale items and store brands, but if there was a $5.00 cake I wanted, I bought it. My grocery bills were $60.00 to $80.00 a day. I justified this by reminding myself that I worked hard all day, always including overtime, and earned a good salary. Besides, this was all I had in my life: working and binging and purging. I had never experienced this much freedom before, and I dealt with it very poorly. I was the wide-eyed, innocent, hungry child left alone in the candy store.

    I quickly learned the layout of each grocery store, and methodically made my way down the aisles. I gave myself permission to purchase whatever foods I wanted, whether it was full-course meals, desserts, or snacks. No food was forbidden or off-limits to me, and I savored every bit of this freedom. At that moment, I did not have to obey the "beast". I could temporarily throw the anorexic rules and schedules out the window. How I hated those restrictions on my life. This was a time when I could pretend to be normal, and to eat all the foods that normal people eat. I remember feeling extremely self-conscious as I stood in the checkout line. The naïve, unknowing comments from cashiers felt like the piercing of a knife blade into my heart. *"You must have a big family at home. What are you going to do with all this food?"* and *"Are you expecting company?"* I made a conscious effort to alternate grocery stores and cashiers. How could I possibly explain buying such large quantities of food two days in a row?

I tried my best to hurry through the checkout, even bagging my own groceries when I could. I do not think I have the capacity to describe the humiliation, embarrassment, and shame that I felt. I replaced these feelings with feelings of anticipation of what I would soon be eating. I locked the groceries and my anorexic fears in the trunk of my car, yet always kept out a special treat that I could eat on the way home.

I also convinced myself that, by exceeding the speed limits, I could get home faster. My first car accident in Florida happened during one of these trips. I was leaving the grocery store, and after looking both ways, pulled out into the break in the median. I honestly did not see the car behind me until it smashed into the back end of my car. I felt all alone, and started crying. I had only lived in Florida for four months, and had not established any friendships yet. I wanted my mother to come and help me, to make everything all right. My true feelings were again buried, and I began worrying about getting home before my ice cream melted. This was delaying my Happy Hour, and I was growing irritable and nervous. The police report was finally completed, and I drove myself home with my heart pounding and my legs shaking.

When I got home, I unloaded the trunk, changed into old clothes, turned on the TV, and started eating. If I was especially weak and tired from days of binging and purging, I sat down on the cold kitchen floor to eat my food, and threw up in a bucket placed next to me. This saved energy and time, since I did not have to keep getting up and running to the bathroom. I waited until the bucket was full before carrying it to the bathroom and flushing the contents down the toilet. At the end of this cycle, I drank an entire gallon of water, taking breaks in-between gulps to throw up. This was how I made sure that my stomach was completely empty, and that I had been cleansed. My next chore was to take the garbage bag full of trash to the dumpster, no matter what time of night it was. I attempted to erase what I had done by cleaning the kitchen and bathroom and scrubbing all the dishes. Once my work was done, I brushed my teeth and took a shower, still trying to cleanse myself of my dirty act. But no matter how hard I scrubbed, I never felt clean. I crawled into bed with a cup of ice cubes to suck on in order to relieve the dryness in my mouth.

My new job was very stressful and demanding. Basically, I was thrown into a position for which I was not prepared. I did not know how to schedule or supervise a department, but I was willing to learn. The more responsibility that I accepted, the more that was expected of me. If I was successful, I thought I would feel secure and proud of myself. It was a fantastic opportunity. The hospital was new and all the departments were starting from the beginning. My new boss was very demanding, yet loving, and a good mentor. He took a chance on me, an inexperienced person with high ambitions. I ended up making a name for myself and got promoted from supervisor to clinical coordinator. But the work was difficult and took all of my energy. My way of rewarding myself was by eating and throwing up after work. I dealt with my loneliness and fears by wrapping my bulimia security blanket around me. I did two modeling jobs in Florida, but never had the faith in myself to pursue it further. I did not think I was as pretty as the other models.

I lived in the apartment for about four months, and severely binged and purged almost every day. I did not get my weight below 100-105 pounds, because I would try to stop vomiting for a few days and eat to the best of my ability. But then the urges to binge and purge would return with a vengeance, and I would fall victim to the bulimic cycle again.

During periods of recovery, I took on the appearance of a chipmunk storing nuts for the winter. I had not yet learned

33

that excessive vomiting caused the salivary glands to swell. These glands secrete saliva and are located on each side of the face surrounding the ear. I did not understand what was happening to me, and was frightened. Two or three days after I had last vomited, my glands would begin to swell and I would look like I had the mumps. I felt ugly and self conscious, and tried to massage my glands with my fingertips to reduce the swelling, but was unsuccessful.

I made an appointment with a physician who tried unsuccessfully to drain my glands. Thin, tiny tubes were inserted through my mouth into my cheeks, and pressure was applied to my glands. However, no fluid came out. When this failed, I endured a study to see if my glands were functioning properly. Radiolucent dye was injected into my glands through the same tubes until I cried in pain. This was done to test the potency of my salivary ducts. The results were negative, and I left the physician's office confused and upset. I just happened to read an article in a medical book that explained that my swollen face was a side effect of bulimia. I was relieved and sad at the same time—relieved that I knew the cause, and sad because I had not been able to stop the "beast". So, I would start living through the "uglies". I would make it a few days without vomiting, but then the urges to self-abuse would hit me again. I would think, *"I am so ugly, I want to bring this swelling down."* But with each relapse, the urges grew stronger and harder to control. Relief from the uglies was too easy: all I had to do was force myself to vomit, and the swelling disappeared.

CHAPTER 12

LIFE-CHANGING DECISIONS

When I was 26 years old, I made a very important, life-changing decision. After years of much thought and careful consideration, I elected to have a tubal ligation. This is the surgical procedure performed to occlude the fallopian tubes to permanently prevent pregnancy. I consulted with numerous physicians, and not one could assure me that I could conceive and deliver a healthy child due to my illnesses. I had known for five or six years that I did not want to have children. I tried furtively to convince myself that I did want to conceive. A normal woman wants to have a family, does she not? My feelings were: (1) I will not allow another human being to suffer as I did with thyroid disease, which is hereditary; (2) I was career-oriented, and did not feel that I could mentally handle raising a child and a fulltime job; and (3) I did not think I was the motherly type, and thought I would fail as a parent. After all, I had already failed in every attempt to beat this disease. I could barely take care of myself—how could I take care of a child? A child deserved a better parent than I could ever be.

The surgery was performed at the hospital where I was employed. I was initially hesitant. This was a very personal and private matter, and all of my co-workers would know. I feared that some of them would not agree with my decision to have this surgery, and would not like me. What kind of person would they think I was? I overcame my fear and pride, and I came through my surgery without complications.

After my surgery, I had taken the advice of co-workers and bought a condo. Again, I was searching for something to make me happy, and rid me of this disease. It did not take long for me to remember that I was unable to live by myself. I reluctantly turned back to binging and purging, and was soon completely absorbed in this destructive behavior. Meanwhile, the stress level at work rose to an unbearable level.

I was on-call two to three weeks out of each month, 24 hours a day, seven days a week. The hospital was preparing to open a neonatal intensive care unit, and our department, Respiratory Care, was heavily involved. This would be an excellent opportunity for career growth and the chance to learn new skills. My responsibilities and liabilities began to overwhelm me. I began to question my desire to be a manager and considered stepping down. I had spent the last three years learning management skills through trial and error. I saw myself as someone who made too many mistakes and was inadequate in her position. I interpreted all constructive criticism as a personal insult.

I was accustomed to sharing my feelings and personal life with my friends and co-workers, perhaps stemming from all the years of psychotherapy. I overlooked the fact that I was now in a supervisory position, and openly discussed my personal life at my job. I was lonely and needed someone to talk to. I was devoting all my time and energy to my work, and had developed a few acquaintances but no close friendships.

I turned to the therapists that I was supervising for friendship and acceptance. I believe that most of them did like me, but I had placed them in a position that they would not be able to fill. I placed my entire sense of self-worth on their opinion of me.

I had been placed in a difficult situation. I had no management experience, and was younger than most of the staff. I was able to understand their feelings of resentment, but unable to protect my feelings from being hurt by their criticism and comments. How could I earn their respect when I was so unsure of myself? Many were more experienced and skillful as therapists than I was. Why would they listen to me?

My confidence in myself as a leader slowly increased as my technical skills increased. I learned many new respiratory procedures, quite a few of them from the therapists themselves. I realized that they did not expect me to know everything. I made many mistakes, and was frequently wrong when they were right. I expected too much of myself, and set myself up for failure and disappointment. Despite all this, I did consider the therapists that I supervised as my friends and family. I tried to make everyone happy, especially when I did the schedule. I desperately wanted them to like me. They were all that I had in my life.

I was very reluctant to reach out to others. I feared that they would reject me because of my strange eating habits and anxiety towards food. If I let them get too close to me, they would discover that I was different than they were. I was not like them. I was not free. I had to obey the strict rules and limitations imposed by the "beast". I envied their freedom and the normalcy of their lives.

My mental and physical deterioration continued until I felt unable to deal with any part of my life. I feared that I was becoming a disappointment and embarrassment to my co-workers and boss. If I could not perform to expectations in my position, then I should not remain in it. I debated making this painful and difficult decision for a few months and tried to keep working. My boss was kind and supportive, and encouraged me to remain on the job and work through this.

I considered my boss to be my friend and teacher. I trusted him, and was grateful for the career opportunity he had given me. He devoted many hours to training and nurturing me, and always defended me. How could I let him down by resigning? What would he think of me? How could I walk away from all this?

I became increasingly nervous and irritable, and developed insomnia. As depression and exhaustion overtook me, I resigned my position at the hospital. I was very unsure of my decision, but knew that I had to do something. I finally confided to my boss that my eating disorder was becoming out of control. I was unable to handle a stressful job and my illness, and I was scared that I was losing my sanity. He hugged me and we promised to keep in touch with each other.

I had saved some money and was financially able to take a six-month break from work. I decided that I could not handle home-ownership right then, so I placed my condo on the market.

I realized that it was time to get serious about stopping the anorexic and bulimic relapses. My physician prescribed Xanax because I was not sleeping much at night and felt emotionally unstable. Xanax is a medicine given to relieve anxiety. It also produces relaxation and mild sedation. Use of these types of drugs can lead to physical and psychological dependence on them. However, I was desperate and willing to try anything. I took one pill before bedtime, and did sleep soundly through the night. As the drug effects wore off during the daytime hours, I would suffer from severe anxiety attacks. My moods were erratic and unpredictable during my month on Xanax. During this nightmare, I signed a contract for the sale of my condo without realizing the financial loss I was incurring. Decisions were nearly impossible for me to make. I was not thinking straight, and did not know who I was. I was frightened and nervous and angry with myself for feeling that way. I called my parents and begged for their help. I flew to Ohio and stayed in my parents' home for one week. Against my doctor's orders, I stopped taking Xanax. Discontinuance of these medicines should be done gradually, decreasing the dosage, and under the careful supervision of a doctor. I was so miserable and distraught that I could not see how I could feel any worse. Once again, I was wrong. The withdrawal symptoms began. Within 12 hours, I experienced consecutive panic attacks filled with extreme anxiety. My head was pounding, my heart was racing, and I was unable to catch my breath. I fidgeted and talked incessantly. I paced back and forth in our living room and began perspiring. When I did try to sit down, my legs would start shaking and bounce up and down. My parents stayed with me, watching helplessly as I suffered. I finally went to bed and slept intermittently for about three hours. When I awoke, I was slightly less nervous and panic-stricken. Within 48 hours, the symptoms had almost completely passed. I was able to think clearer, and sleep through the night.

I returned to Florida a scared little girl who moved back in with Jim. I was desperately searching for peace and security in my life.

CHAPTER 13

INTRODUCTION TO PROZAC

I finally confessed my anorexic/bulimic relapse to my physician and asked him if I could start on Prozac, an antidepressant. I had been reading a new book on treatment for eating disorders. It had mentioned that medications were now available to help control chemical imbalances associated with eating disorders. By stabilizing the levels of serotonin in the brain, the compulsive urges to binge and purge would decrease and, in some case, even go away. Could this finally be my cure? Was this too good to be true? I jumped on the bandwagon, feeling encouraged and excited. I was willing to try anything; I was desperate. I looked to the medicine for hope, even though it was a very new treatment for eating disorders. I started taking a low dose (20 mg.) of Prozac. The exact dosage for treatment of eating disorders had not yet been established. My moods began to stabilize, and my self-confidence increased. I felt like I could handle things better while on Prozac. The medicine felt like a safety net, one that would catch me before I fell into the pit of darkness. I have been taking Prozac for 4-5 years now, and plan to continue on it.

The year before Jim and I got married, I went almost an entire year without binging and vomiting. I was taking 20 mg. of Prozac then, and I weighed about 105 pounds. For about the first eight months of this stretch, I ate the exact same thing every day, adhering to my anorexic rituals. I was afraid I would relapse if I ate anything even slightly different. I was very proud of myself for not throwing up during this time. I was feeling better physically than I had in a long time. I was eating a grapefruit for lunch, and plain tortilla shells with warm milk for dinner. These were my safe, non-threatening foods. Each had to be eaten at a certain time of day. If I missed my schedule, I felt frightened and lost. This led to a panic attack, which subsequently led to a bulimic relapse.

I had stopped taking Prozac and tried two other antidepressants prior to my second hospitalization. My doctor and I had both felt unsure that Prozac was still helping my obsessive-compulsive feelings. I experienced no relief from the other medicines, and my depression grew darker and deeper. Prozac is the only medicine that has helped to ease and, even occasionally, take away the urges to binge and vomit or starve myself. It will usually keep me stable so that I can deal with problems in my life. My first experiences with Prozac were some of the best times of my life. I realize that there have not been studies done to show the effects of long-term use of Prozac, but I refuse to let that worry me. One benefit that I get from the drug is feeling that I have more self-confidence and can handle the ups and downs of my life. In the beginning, I experienced the "happy high" period, during which I felt my outlook brighten. Peace and happiness entered my life. But that faded away—it was not a happy pill, but more of a coping tool. I have been told that I will probably be on Prozac for the rest of my life, along with Synthroid. I accept this, and believe that I require this medicine. I am able to deal with the side effects. Primarily, I have headaches and some flu-like symptoms. Occasionally, I have low-grade fevers, am anxious, and experience daytime sleepiness. But these symptoms do not approach the side effects of binging and purging.

And, I know that I am worse when I am not taking Prozac. A sinking feeling overwhelms me. There is no ray of hope, or light at the end of the tunnel. I used to be able to tell friends and co-workers that I thought I had my eating disorder under control. It was not until I came to Florida that it got far out of control, and caused such destruction in my life.

CHAPTER 14

RELAPSING DURING THE HOLIDAYS

The holidays, which should be a time of joy and happiness, have always been difficult for me. This is not only because food is a large part of the celebration, but also because I was always very nervous and uncomfortable around my family during these times. I became angry with myself for feeling that way, and the anger would, in turn, contribute to the holiday relapses. It was a lose/lose situation for me. If I avoided all the food, I could abstain from binging and purging. However, I would realize I was depriving myself and think, *"It's not fair that I can't eat, too",* and *"Poor me, I want to be normal like everyone else."* Of course, the baked goods and dinners are always very abundant, extravagant, and delicious around Thanksgiving and Christmas. I always volunteered to work and did work most of the holidays as a way to avoid these miserable feelings and uncomfortable situations. I honestly wanted to be with my family, and I hope they were not offended when I was not.

I remember my first Christmas in Florida. I was on-call at the hospital, and could not fly home to be with my family. Jim and I barely knew one another, and were still only platonic roommates. He had made plans to spend Christmas with his friends. The urges to binge and purge had returned and were growing stronger. I knew that I was going to give in, and started planning the horrible event.

I decided to rent a room at a hotel on the beach. I convinced myself, Jim, and my aunt that I was going on a mini-vacation, and doing something nice for myself. I have always loved the beach, walking along the shoreline as the salt water caressed my feet and ankles. The pleasure of feeling the warm, soft sand between my toes, and the peaceful sound of the waves breaking on the shore, was the closest I could come to experiencing a shred of peace in my mind.

I booked a room for Christmas Eve, packed an overnight bag, and drove to the beach. I was filled with anticipation and dread. I could hardly wait to eat all the scrumptious, forbidden foods that my heart desired, yet I dreaded the mental and physical pain that would follow. I was all too familiar with the self-disgust, shame, and disappointment that would ensue the following morning.

I drove fast, wanting to devote the greatest amount of time to binging and purging. I believed that I could temporarily shut out the real world, and almost disappear. More importantly, I did not have to acknowledge the fact that I was all alone for Christmas. I thought that anyone who chose to do this to herself did not deserve to be with her family. Why hurt them too? Why show them how ill I really was?

I stopped at a grocery store on the way to the beach

and purchased my favorite forbidden foods, foods that were soon to be "recycled," as someone once said to me. I checked in at the front desk, and quickly carried my groceries from my car to the room. I locked the door, closed the blinds, and changed into old clothes. I did not want my good clothes to be splattered with vomit stains.

At about 10:00 p.m., I was finally finished. My throat was raw and sore, and my eyes were bloodshot. I was unable to stop my body from shivering, and the tears from rolling down my cheeks. I was disgusted by the image reflected in the bathroom mirror. I was looking at an ugly, undesirable girl with dried vomit on her face and in her hair. Why had I done this to myself? Why had I *wanted* to do this to myself?

After I cleaned myself up, I carried my bag of trash and the old clothes I had worn to the dumpster. I disposed of my clothes in a futile attempt to separate this filthy act completely from myself. I did not want to look at those clothes again, only to be reminded of how bad I had been.

I returned to my room and curled up in my bed. I was soon overwhelmed with feelings of loneliness, sadness, and despair. I missed my family so much, and longed to be with them. I pictured them sitting side-by-side in the church pew at the candlelight Christmas Eve service. Why could I not be there, too? Why could I not show them how much I loved them?

During an argument many years ago, my father had referred to me as "*the bad seed.*" It was said out of anger, and he apologized later. I knew he did not mean it, and that he loved me very much. I, too, have said many painful things out of anger, and I wish I could take them back. Nevertheless, I thought of myself as the bad seed or black sheep of the family from then on.

I began to pray, and promised God that this would be the last time I binged and purged. What a beautiful time to quit this behavior, on the observed birthday of Jesus Christ. I could tell everyone that I had become clean and had made a fresh, new start on Christmas Day. It was this thread of hope, not sugar plums, that danced in my head as I slept that Christmas Eve night.

CHAPTER 15

FALLING IN LOVE WITH JIM

When Jim and I met, I was 24 and he was 36. We were opposites in every sense of the word. However, I was very attracted to him. He was not what I had previously considered to be my type at all. He had just experienced a broken engagement and was very distraught by that, believing that any woman he became involved with would eventually hurt him emotionally. I took this as a challenge. I wanted to see what would happen between us.

Jim was probably the first and only man that completely rejected me. He made it clear that he did not want a relationship, and yet I pursued it. I guess I felt a connection between us. It was exciting and different. I was so wrapped up in my demanding job that I had very little time left over for myself. Still I felt like a stranger in Florida, and had not developed close friendships. The weekend fun and companionship that Jim had to offer was enough for me. During the week we hardly spoke to one another and lived as platonic roommates. Very gradually and cautiously, we became involved. However, neither one of us was emotionally ready for a relationship, and we broke up one month later.

A year passed and Jim and I remained just friends and roommates. Then the fire was rekindled and we became re-involved. However, I decided that I was going to play it cool this time, and let him pursue me. I was determined to stop chasing him, and stop making myself so readily available to him. I followed my own advice, and we eventually found ourselves in a weekend-only romance. The irony is that the weekends were the only time that Jim would drink alcohol. He drank rum and cokes on Friday and Saturday nights, and after playing golf on Saturday afternoons. He was also a cigarette smoker. The person I fell in love with was the person he became after having a few drinks. It was the only time he would openly share his feelings with me. He became talkative, pleasant and was very nice to me. And that was the person with whom I fell in love. During the week, Jim hardly spoke to me. He treated me as a casual friend. Then the weekend would come around and it was time to be a couple again. I began to feel that I was a convenience, and I was tired of feeling rejected by him during the week. However, I realized that I had initiated this affair, and entered into it with my eyes wide open. I had only myself to blame. As I mentioned previously, Jim was highly critical of me. I recognized obsessive/compulsive traits in him. I saw myself in him. I had compassion for him, because I knew that he did not want to be this way. Jim was an extreme perfectionist. There were all kinds of rules and regulations in his home that I had to follow. For example, if it was raining, I could not pull the car into the garage because water would drip all over the floor. Then, when I did pull it in, I had to dry both the car and garage floor off immediately. I had to vacuum the carpets every seven days, or Jim would become angry, grab the vacuum, and do it himself. He was very particular about the way I washed clothes. Many of his rules and ideas were useful and intelligent. Some of his expectations were things that I needed to learn. Our home was always the prettiest and cleanest on the block.

Jim worked every day delivering medical equipment. When he came home, he always worked outside in the yard, clipping the hedges or the bushes, mowing—for at least an hour every single night before he came inside. He worked very, very hard on our first home by painting the walls, stripping the floors, and remodeling. He put a lot of sweat into it; he wanted it to have a high resale value. One of the first things my father said to me concerning Jim was, *"He keeps a beautiful house. He would be a good man to get a ring from"*

The problem was that he expected me to be as perfect as he was trying to be, and became frustrated with me if I was not. If I accidentally dinged the wall with the vacuum cleaner, he saw it as an offensive action taken against him. How could I do that to him? Did I have no sense of love, no sense of respect for his home or for him? I would stand there with my mouth open, confused and dejected, knowing that it had been an accident. I started to believe that I would never be good enough for him.

   During this time, my aunt passed away. She had been chronically ill for years, and I was blessed to have been able to spend time with her and get to know her. I was even able to have her admitted to the hospital where I worked so she could receive better care from skilled doctors whom I knew. I always felt that I did not do enough for her, but I treasured our time together. She enjoyed getting out of her house for a while, even if we only went grocery shopping. I loved her dearly, and Jim did too. She had a special place in her heart for Jim, and always said that he was a good and decent man.

   My parents did not like Jim at first, because he had been drinking the night they had met. However, my father did say that he was a talented housekeeper. Jim had lived alone as a bachelor for many years. His immediate family consists of only him and his sister. His mother had a son from a previous marriage with whom we have grown much closer over the past few years. Jim's father died from a heart attack when Jim was only 14, and his mother passed away when he was about 24. Jim endured the pain of watching his mother die from cancer, an image he will never forget. I can only imagine how difficult that was. He says now that he wishes he had spent more time with her, and had been more loving and supportive. He did not know how to handle the pain and remorse he felt during the weeks preceding her death, so he chose not to be at home much with her. He regrets that choice every day of his life.

   Jim attended college at his mother's request, and earned a business degree before her death. He worked at different jobs until he started delivering medical equipment. He was a conscientious and reliable employee. He told me openly that he had lived alone for a long time and was set in his ways. Unfortunately, in the back of my mind, I was trying to change him. I wanted to make things better for him, to be the woman who could change his life for the better. I could be the one woman he could trust, and his life would improve with me in it. I could show him how to love. What I overlooked was that he never asked me to take on this noble cause. I never asked or received his permission to change his life. Our relationship fell together in little pieces at a time. There came a time when I finally knew that a weekend-only romance was not enough for me. I wanted to be his girlfriend. If we were going to be a couple on the weekends, why could we not officially be boyfriend-girlfriend? I was not asking him to marry me, but I wanted a commitment and some sense of security. I thought this was fair. He initially was hesitant, but then agreed. I already knew that I was in love with him, but did not feel comfortable enough to share my feelings with him.

I remember we had a misunderstanding on Valentine's Day, which was very painful for me. I once again experienced feelings of rejection and humiliation. Jim and I had made plans to go out and have a romantic dinner that evening. I bought a tight-fitting and very sexy little black dress, and was determined to knock Jim's socks off. Valentine's day had fallen on a Saturday, and Jim and I spent almost every Saturday night with our friend Paul. Jim and Paul played golf during the day, came home to shower and change, and the three of us would head out for dinner and drinks for the guys. I was the designated driver since I did not drink. I enjoyed being the only girl, and hanging out with the boys. I felt special. I waited in anticipation for the end of the evening, when Jim and I would be alone. Remember, I fell in love with the person Jim was when he was drinking. He would want to be with me, and would be nice to me.

I anxiously waited for Jim to come home that night, and kept nervously adjusting my little black dress. Jim finally came home and was in the shower when the doorbell rang. I opened the door, and there stood Paul, whose first words were, *"What are you all dressed up for, Lauren?"* I wanted to dig a hole and bury myself in it.

I made up an excuse to tell Paul, and walked to Jim's bedroom to confront him. He had not understood that this was supposed to be a formal and special night out for just the two of us. I was very hurt. The three of us went out anyway, but I barely spoke to Jim. It was the only way I could hold back my tears and frustration. When we returned home, I went directly to my room, closed the door, and cried into my pillow. Jim came in later and tried to explain, but we were on two entirely different wavelengths. Shortly after that, I bought my condo and moved out of Jim's home. The Valentine's Day disaster and my assertion of independence brought Jim to the realization that he had developed deep feelings for me. I could afford to buy my own home, and was financially able to take care of myself. He told me that he loved me as much as I loved him. It seems that it has always taken some monumental event for Jim to realize and admit his true feelings for me. He was a closed book who shelved his emotions. For example, he never used to talk about his parents or his childhood. We are at the point now where he will talk about them both openly and comfortably. The changes that Jim and I have gone through have been phenomenal. Thanks to God, we have both matured greatly.

CHAPTER 16

RELAPSING AND LYING

One of my relapses had a detrimental and profound effect on our relationship. I was afraid to admit to myself and to Jim that I had given in to the disease, so I lied to hide the truth. I wanted desperately for something else to be medically wrong with me. This is when I had numerous diagnostic tests performed. I did not think I would deserve or should receive any sympathy for admitting that it was an anorexic/bulimic relapse. I thought that would be admitting that I was a weak failure. People would still love me if I said it was something else. How do you tell someone, *"Yes, this disease is still in my life,"* or *"No, I still cannot stop throwing up."?* I lied to myself and to others, among them my primary care physician. I became so ill that I ended up on home intravenous therapy. Jim was very supportive during this time. He mixed and hung my IV bags for me

47

and was very compassionate. A "normal" illness, not self-induced, was something he could accept and be sympathetic towards. It would not change his opinion of me. Jim has always been the one who drove to the drugstore, no matter what time of day, to get me my medicines. It was only a year prior to this that I had told him I had been anorexic as a teenager. He told me right then that if I ever relapsed back into anorexia that he would leave me, and I believed him. I know now that he would not have left, but I did not know it then.

My mother spent a week with us during that time helping to care for me and giving Jim the chance to take a weekend trip with his friends. I insisted that he go even though I was very sick. I bore a tremendous amount of guilt for the pain I was inflicting on him. At least one of us could temporarily take a break from the illness. I eventually convinced him to take the trip without me. Mom's opinion of Jim began to change, because she saw how much he loved me by the way he took care of me. I believe that, in his heart, he thought he could take care of me, and that he would be able to cure me of any disease. He has said numerous times that he wanted to take my sickness on, and that he could fight it for me. It was a fight he felt confident he could win.

I was very envious of Jim because he had stopped smoking and drinking so easily. He is one of the very few people I know that has given up an addictive habit without suffering from any withdrawal effects. As a respiratory therapist, I have seen the damage caused by cigarettes to my patients' lungs. Jim does not seem to carry that addictive gene in his brain. He said smoking had only been a habit for him, something to do. I admire him and am very proud of him for this accomplishment. Yet I think that this is why it is so difficult for him to understand the powerful forces behind my addiction. If he could successfully stop, why couldn't I? How could it be so much harder for me? I tried in vain to make Jim understand the horrible, compulsive thoughts in my head, but every attempt resulted in a new argument and a new wall rising up between us.

I agonized over the best way to tell Jim the truth while

continuing to hide my anorexia. When he was working, I was home eating and throwing up. I learned ways to hide my destructive behavior and became sneaky, deceitful, and manipulative. I hated the person I was becoming. I have always tried to be an honest person, but when I am in a binge and purge cycle, lying comes so easily. It does not matter why I was lying. I was still looking into Jim's eyes and deceiving him. How could he possibly forgive me for causing him such mental anguish? How could he ever trust me again? He did not tolerate lying and, in fact, had some friends who had lied to him who were not his friends anymore. How could I stop the lies without losing him?

    I felt that I did not deserve to live at home with Jim, so I stayed with our friend, Paul, for about two weeks. Also, I knew that it was upsetting Jim for him to see me so thin and ill. I thought that I would not have to bear the cross of guilt and deceit if he did not have to look at me. I could not tolerate myself for what I was doing to Jim. One day while I was living at Paul's, my car broke down and I had called Paul to come and get me. I was in the middle of a busy, stressful workday at my new job, and felt emotionally unstable. Right there, in the middle of the street, I grabbed Paul's hands and started sobbing. I told him the truth. Actually, I told his feet the truth, because I was too ashamed to look into his eyes. He was so kind, saying that we were going to get help for me, and that everything would be fine. He asked me if I wanted him to tell Jim, and I said no. I knew that I was the only candidate for that job.

    So, I went home and confessed to Jim. My heart was beating so fast, and I was nervously pacing the floor. It did not go over well at all. He was furious, and I cannot blame him for feeling that way. I had lied to him. It took him almost two years to trust me again. Lying would become an issue when we had disagreements and arguments. He would say, *"I can't trust you. How do I know you're telling the truth? You lied before."* I never had an answer for him and wondered if he would ever forgive me.

CHAPTER 17

COMBINING MARRIAGE AND AN EATING DISORDER

Time passed and Jim and I eventually became engaged. I had been very demanding concerning our relationship. I remember driving to Jim's work one day and telling him that I wanted to be engaged. I felt that I was being exploited, and that if our relationship was important to him, it was time to take the next step. At that time, we had been together for five or six years. Jim was scared and hesitant, yet I kept pushing him. I made the choice to pursue him all by myself. If I was setting myself up for misery, then so be it. I would have only myself to blame. I had suddenly developed some self-confidence, and believed that I deserved his appreciation and love. I do not think I knew how to handle feeling confident and assertive. It was brand new and frightening territory to me.

The following year was filled with frustration and doubt, because Jim did not want to announce our engagement. He was afraid that it would fall apart just like his previous engagement. He did not want to look like a fool twice. He was still very unsure and hesitant, and that bothered me immensely. We had many talks and arguments about it, and he never seemed to let me forget that I was the one who wanted the engagement, and had pushed so hard for it. There were a couple of times, I remember, when I even gave the ring back. I was the one who proposed anyway, who caused the damage, so I would just put things back the way they were. But then he would say that he did not want to be without me, and that he simply needed more time. I always saw through Jim's tough, protective exterior to his gentle, loving heart. I believed in him, and I loved him dearly. There was never an issue of anyone else. That is another way in which the Lord has blessed Jim and me. We have never had a problem with infidelity. We were always loyal to each other, and trusted one another in this regard. I never doubted his faithfulness to me.

During this time, I was very healthy and I did not have a

relapse for almost an entire year. Even though I ate my scheduled meals at scheduled times, I did not throw up. I started looking and feeling better, and I was learning to like myself. Men paid attention to me again, and complimented me. I was asked out on dates by the men who fixed the windshield on my car and tiled our bathroom floor. I never went looking for attention. It found me. I found the comments of these men so flattering and uplifting that I came close to having an affair.

Jim did not compliment me. He was not the kind of person to say *"you're beautiful, you're pretty."* He also believed that even though I was healthy, I was still too thin. Yet here were two men who were telling me that I was not too thin, and that Î was a beautiful, sexy woman. Could they be right?

That was quite a temptation for me. It was good that it happened, and I realize why I was so vulnerable. My self-esteem was low, and the attention helped to boost it. It helped me to see myself as a strong, beautiful woman, something I had not seen in many years, if ever.

I cannot say why I always came back to Jim, but I did. I put far too much emphasis on what Jim thought of me. I placed him in a position that I doubt anyone could fulfill. I was placing my whole self worth on whether or not he came home and said *"good girl, Lauren, you cleaned the floor just right,"* or *"good girl, Lauren, you did this right,"* or *"good girl, Lauren, you look pretty today."* What he did say was never enough, and it left me feeling sad and dejected.

Very gradually, during the last month or so before we got married, I started eating different foods at dinnertime. I discovered that I really liked food cooked out on the grill. At this time, Jim was more verbally abusive, and obsessed with the way things had to be in the house. However, the more I allowed him to hurt my feelings, the less I hurt myself. I believed that Jim had a good heart, and I loved him deeply. I did not doubt his love for me, and I certainly could have left at any time. Yet I always stayed.

Meanwhile, Jim had curtailed his drinking, and had also quit smoking. We were going to be married. Then one night before the wedding, we had cooked pork chops on the grill. They were still a little pink inside, but we ate them anyway. Over the next few days, I became ill and genuinely could not keep food down. That was something else with my very tight anorexic schedule. No matter what illness I got, even if it was just the flu or a cold, I could not handle it. To me, being sick meant falling off the wagon. I could only let myself be sick if it was self-induced. That was the only way I could justify feeling ill. And once again, I fell into the dark, dismal pit of relapse.

We had a small wedding in our home, with only our immediate families in attendance. I wore my mother's dress, and it was beautiful. We honeymooned at Walt Disney World and enjoyed ourselves until, once again, the anorexia "beast" returned to ruin my happiness.

I do not want to paint an unflattering picture of Jim. They say that you marry someone like your father and, in many ways, Jim is like my father. I always know what time he will be home, and where he is. We both place importance on saving money, and share similar long-term financial goals. He is an honest man, and he has never cheated on me. I know that in his own way, in his heart, he loves me more than anything in this world.

I tried to live by most of Jim's rules. I thought that by doing so, maybe some of my anorexic rules would disappear. And, if he was mentally punishing me, maybe I would not have to punish myself through eating and vomiting. These thoughts were always in my head, and I think that is why I tolerated the times when Jim treated me poorly.

Jim lost his job a month after we got married. He had worked at the same job for about 12 years. He had been miserable working there the past couple of years. This led to stress that he internalized and later took out on me. I had fallen into a relapse, and was battling the strongest compulsive urges that I had ever felt. They overpowered me so much that if I had been in a car, and my mother had been standing in the street, I would have run her over to get to the grocery store to buy food. How could I think such awful thoughts? My efforts at recovery had been unsuccessful. Jim wanted to sell our house and move out of town. We had been trying to sell the house for a few months, because the neighborhood had changed. He wanted to move to the town where my brother-in-law lived. He had not checked out the area and did not have a job there, but was sure that this was what he wanted. He wanted us to make a fresh start in a new town, and leave our problems behind. During that time, my professional life was very settled and I was content. I was with a company that gave respiratory therapy in extended care facilities and rehabilitation centers. I was well liked at work, where I had many friends and people who loved and cared for me. I had requested a transfer but it did not work out. Jim and I endured many arguments and times of sheer frustration over the next year.

We eventually sold the house, and Jim agreed that we could rent a home for one year, then see what developed. He hated paying rent, and soon decided that we should buy a house. I was afraid to do so, and had to put my foot down and tell him that he needed to find a job before I would even consider purchasing a home with him. During this time, I was working two jobs, by choice. I did the same type of work for another respiratory therapy company. Jim never asked or forced me to work an additional job. I was hoping that working two jobs might be the answer to making the illness stop. The long hours and extra income might help me like and be proud of myself. Then the illness might go away. If I made more money, I would like myself and become a good person.

I always wanted to give Jim everything, and I think that is why I worked a second job for so long. I knew he was unhappy with the way I looked, and that he was not sexually attracted to me. However, I thought that by earning extra money I could make him love and accept me, and he would be able to overlook my appearance. I realize now that working this much was not the way to conquer the illness. It just replaced the disease with work. It was not a permanent answer, and did not last.

Jim tried to find a job by looking through want ads and making telephone calls. I had difficulty believing that he was putting enough effort into his search, although I understood that he felt he deserved time off. He had worked

53

steadily for many years. He did have a good pension from his previous job. We re-invested this in an IRA. However, I always wondered whether he considered my financial support to be a debt I owed for the times I had lied to him and hid the anorexia. He always denied that, but I felt in my heart that it was probably true.

Jim was unemployed for a year and a half. This was very difficult for both of us. Some of the employers to whom he applied would not even return his calls. He had certain things that he wanted to do, and others that he did not want to do. Meanwhile, my frustration built because I wanted to tell him that if he really loved me, he would want to be supporting me. He would want to be working. I held my tongue, because I did not want to be a nag. I wanted him to see me as a supportive wife who "stands by her man." I did not care where he worked as long as he was helping to pay our bills. I had supported him for too long.

These troubling times progressed from bad to worse. While I tried not to nag or push Jim, a part of me felt rejected. I wondered if I had the right to push him. Jim initially received three months severance pay. This was followed by six months of unemployment compensation. I thank God for those financial gifts. When they ran out, I began asking myself, *"why doesn't he want to work to provide for us?"* We were lucky that we had savings in the bank, and that my jobs paid well. We could temporarily survive financially without his working. But that horrible thought always returned: was he trying to pay me back for all those times I lied about the illness, covered it up, and all the enjoyment we missed out on because I was sick?

I was very thin, and my weight continued to plummet. I weighed 90 or 95 pounds at the time of our wedding. For the first time ever during my protracted illness, I was weighing in the 70's. The more I binged and vomited, the less weight I was able to maintain. Jim liked bigger, healthy-looking women. I had always been too thin for him, even when we first met. I remember overhearing him say this to his friends. I felt sad. I believe he did try to love me as I was.

It was very difficult for Jim to understand this disease.

Why would someone want to hurt herself, want to destroy herself, and have these awful urges inside her? Did he not know that I hated these urges and feelings, and would do anything to get rid of them and be able to be nice to myself? I weep bitterly over all the living I missed during those years of sickness and captivity. I cannot help but feel that I was robbed of that part of my life. I wish I could have it back.

Eventually, Jim found work. He moved lawns for a retirement community, and later found a job making cabinets. He has worked at the cabinet shop for the past year, and I am very proud of him. I happened to see an ad for a cabinetmaker in the newspaper and mentioned it to Jim. I thought that it could be something at which he would excel since he is very meticulous and detail-oriented. I have always believed in him more than he has believed in himself. I told anyone who would listen that he was an excellent worker, loyal and dependable.

Finding the cabinet job happened during another recovery period for me. We had lived in the rental house for a little over a year, and had just found a beautiful home to buy. It was only a few miles away from the rental house, and had everything for which we had been looking. We fell in love with it immediately.

I prayed for guidance to help us decide whether or not to purchase the house. I wanted to be sure that our marriage and his job were secure first. Guidance from the Lord made our decision easy to make. Things fell into place beautifully. For three to four months we truly enjoyed one another and our new home. Intimacy and passion returned to our marriage, and we finally felt like newlyweds. The house was beautiful and even had a swimming pool. The previous owners were very neat and clean, and had kept the house in excellent shape. We both worked hard on our new home. It really did not need much touching up, but Jim's desire for perfection manifested itself. He found some areas for improvement. We painted the insides of the closets, the garage, and the outside of the house. Jim landscaped our yard, and we both put a lot of labor, sweat and tears into it. Surprisingly, we worked well as a team. Jim let me do some painting and hardly criticized my work. He complimented me and had patience with me. He was genuinely appreciative of my help and really tried to show this to me.

I know that if Jim could, he would fight this illness for me. He does try to show compassion towards me. Sometimes his love is expressed as an insult. I know he does not mean this. I have to learn to stop taking things so personally. I have to learn to stop taking his jovial teasing so seriously. I also need to be strong. There are times when I need to stand up to him, and I am learning to do that.

I have always deprived myself of material things, and have great difficulty spending money on myself. I am probably one of the few women alive who hates to shop. If I have to shop anywhere, I shop at the thrift stores. I really do not feel that I need materials things. That is where Jim steps in, tells me to get what I need, and to be nice to myself. He says, *"I want you to look good and feel good. You deserve it. I want you to be healthy. Please just get healthy."* I know that he wants that for me more than anything else in the world.

Three or four years ago, when I first met my brother-in-law and sister-in-law, Cliff and Darlene, the first thing that Darlene said to me was that they could not believe the changes in Jim, how he was smiling and happy. She believed it was because he and I were together and in such a close, loving relationship. That was very special to hear, especially coming from them. I needed to hear that I was also bringing Jim happiness, not just frustration and worries.

Jim and I have had a very tumultuous, problem-filled nine years together. We have had good and bad times, and have both changed so much. I think that he needed me to love him unconditionally. I needed him for stabilization and moderation, to show me that work was not the most important part of my life. He was able to leave work at the office at the end of the day. He taught me that being the boss will not bring happiness, that having a title does not make one a better person. And he taught me to have patience with myself.

CHAPTER 18

MY SECOND HOSPITALIZATION

A severe relapse in my condition led to my second hospitalization. Due to the severity of this particular bulimic relapse, I got desperate enough that I confided in a nurse-practitioner at the nursing home where I worked. After many internal debates, I convinced myself to try another psychiatrist. I no longer believed that psychiatric treatment was the answer for my eating disorder. I did not believe that I had been helped by it, and I certainly was not cured. However, I was at the point where the disease had become an overpowering addiction that I could not fight alone. I did not have the necessary weapons in my possession. The urges to binge and vomit were severe, and I was out of control.

The practitioner I spoke with referred me to a psychiatrist. I made the appointment, canceled it, and eventually called back and rescheduled. Reluctantly and fearfully, I drove to the appointment. My husband chose not to go with me. Neither one of us was prepared for what was going to happen when I walked in the office door that day. I have always been very naïve and trusting. I walked in thinking that I would have a session with the psychiatrist, and probably start seeing him weekly as an outpatient. Here again, I was trying to control my therapy by making my own rules.

I met the psychiatrist, and thought he was a very nice man. My skepticism and fears began to fade away, and I felt comfortable confiding in him. Maybe I should give psychiatric care one more try. Maybe he was the one doctor who would set me free from my captivity. We talked for about 30 minutes. My main reason for not being re-hospitalized was the awful experience that I had as a teenager in the psychiatric ward. In addition, my health insurance company considered anorexia to be a pre-existing condition, and refused to cover any hospitalization costs. I explained this to the physician, and he immediately called the

57

insurance company. To my surprise, he told me that they had agreed to override the pre-existing clause due to the fact that I was in a life and death situation. The physician informed them that my condition was critical, and that I could die without extensive and immediate treatment. I weighed about 75 pounds then. Each year this illness continued, my body got weaker and sicker, and I was not able to handle the painful self-abuse for as long a time as before. The after-effects of each relapse became more severe, and my body and mind paid stiffer penalties.

My financial excuse for not being hospitalized had been stripped from me, leaving me feeling naked. I told the physician that I wanted to think about being admitted, but he denied my request. The decision was already made, and I had not been given a choice. I was Baker-acted, meaning that I was sent to a psychiatric hospital against my will. This is perfectly legal for a physician to do if the life of a patient is at risk. I understand that he did it for my own good, but it was another frightening and humiliating experience for me. I was allowed to call my husband, and pleaded and begged for him to rescue me. Meanwhile, four policemen came to the physician's office, placed me in the backseat of a patrol car, and escorted me to the hospital. I did not fight, but went voluntarily. I felt so alone and afraid, like an animal being led to the slaughter. I had no idea what was going to happen to me, and could not stop crying. As the police car approached the tollbooth, I looked out the window and recognized the toll taker. I curled up in a tight ball and buried my head between my legs in an attempt to hide myself from him. But it was too late. I will never forget the look on his face as he stared at me that day.

I was put in the locked unit of the hospital the first night, and I was scared. All I wanted to do was go home. To my surprise, I was not given any aggressive, life-sustaining treatment such as IV's or tube feedings. I remember being touched and kissed by a male patient, which increased my feelings of despair and fear. I asked him nicely to leave me alone, and he did. He was not angry or violent, and I did not believe that he wanted to hurt or scare me. In fact, when I started crying, he almost did, too. I told my doctor about this incident the following morning, but he did not seem concerned at all, and I wondered if he even believed me. Again here I was, the only anorexic in a locked psychiatric unit. When I agreed to stay at the hospital voluntarily, I was transferred to another unit and given more freedom. The nurses and technicians did not monitor me closely. I managed to take extra snacks from the kitchen area, eat them and vomit, and no one knew. I only did this once, on the second day of my stay at the hospital. I think I was only weighed a couple of times during my stay, even though I requested to be weighed almost every day.

One very beneficial thing that this physician did was to put me back on Prozac and at a higher dose. He observed doctors prescribed 60-80 mg. for those with eating disorders. Nobody had told me that my dosage was too low.

I do not believe that anorexia stems from depression. For me, it was just the opposite. I only found myself depressed when the anorexia/bulimia was out of control, and when I was actively hurting myself. Those were my darkest hours, when I felt hopeless, angry, and disgusted with myself. Otherwise, I could have handled anything and everything calmly and rationally.

At the hospital, we were divided into Group A and Group B for therapy sessions. Jim went to one or two of these with me, and he and I also had a joint session with my physician. This was the second time that the idea of Jim contributing to my relapses was placed in my head. Jim had been unemployed for the past few months. We were told that his unemployment, and his emotional treatment of me, had caused me to rebel against him by abusing myself (to be discussed in a later chapter). That was a real eye-opener. I always wondered if my husband had really wanted to marry me, or if he had done so just to appease me. I was the one anxious to get married. This was a frequent topic in our arguments with one another. I loved him, and had always wanted to be his wife. At that time he wanted to move out of town and start over. I was advised that this would not be a healthy move for me, since I had a good life here, with a secure job and good friends. Why would I even consider moving to where he did not even have a job? Why trade the known for the unknown? Jim was very good to me during my hospitalization. He visited me daily and ate lunch and dinner with me when he could. I was released from the hospital after one week. I continued outpatient therapy sessions with my physician, and tried to practice the new life-coping skills I had acquired. I suffered a moderate bulimic relapse, but quickly got back on track, where I stayed for about four months. Unfortunately, this was a very stressful time for me. About a week after I was released from the hospital, I started receiving bills and letters from my health insurance company, stating that they should not have paid my hospital bill because my condition was pre-existing. I received almost one bill per day over the next four months. I began to dread getting the mail, and did not understand why this company was being so cruel to me. It was extremely upsetting. I was simply trying to get well and return to work. They denied ever saying that they would override the pre-existing condition clause and cover my hospitalization. They wrote to the hospital asking for a refund, and the hospital actually gave the money back to them, leaving me with a bill of $7,000. I made numerous phone calls to the insurance company, begging and pleading my case; but it was to no avail. My physician tried intervening on my behalf, but they refused to change their minds. We retained a lawyer and tried unsuccessfully to pursue the matter. Finally, I reached the point of realizing that fighting the company was causing me extreme mental anguish and interfering with my recovery. I had lost the strength to keep fighting.

    I had recently become a Christian, and was trying to live my life the way God wanted. I knew that I needed to forgive the health insurance company, move forward, and not look back. So, that is what I did. Jim and I were able to pay the bills with money from our savings, but we were left financially strapped. It was very hard to do, but once I forgave the company, I had a sense of peace. It had been quite an ordeal—all the phone calls back and forth, all the nastiness and unwillingness to help on their part. I realized that patients do not take precedent over money. It hurt deep in my soul to learn that my health and feelings did not matter. It gave me a totally new feeling for the trials people experience with their own health insurance companies.

As I had mentioned, I suffered a bulimic relapse after I was released from the hospital. My psychiatrist wanted me to be re-admitted to the psychiatric hospital, but I refused. He said he could not treat me if I was not re-hospitalized for a period of at least two weeks, so we split very amicably. I still value him as a physician and have nothing negative to say about him. One of the best things that he did for me, while I was his patient, was to uncover recurring problems with what was left of my thyroid gland. I had told him that many times when the anorexia/bulimia got out of control, it was because my thyroid levels were not right. He ordered a blood test, and one of my levels was not within normal limits. He increased the dosage of my Synthroid, and I began to notice the change in my body. I felt more human. My head did not hurt as badly, and my depression began to lift. Through a blood test, the thyroid stimulating hormone is checked to see whether or not the thyroid gland is receiving enough Synthroid medicine. I can be either hypo or hyper, under or over the norm. The test definitely showed that I was hypo, meaning that I was not taking enough medicine. This in itself can cause depression and many physiological problems. An untreated thyroid can cause one to believe that she is crazy, or mentally unbalanced. One comes to believe that they are out of control and out of touch with reality. I do not know if I can accurately describe it. The first warning sign for me is head pain. It is true that severe head pain does come from eating and vomiting—I will not deny that at all—but its origin can stem from an unbalanced thyroid as well.

CHAPTER 19

SEARCHING FOR ANSWERS

I continued my quest for that one treatment that would stop the disease, that one special dosage change, doctor, or hospitalization. There had to be something that would take all this pain away. During the times that I was having the bulimic relapses, I would be so disgusted with myself that I would, on occasion, purposely spend the night in a hotel. I did not feel that I deserved to stay in my own home when I was vomiting. I would tell my husband that I did not have the right to lie next to him in bed. I could not stay in my own home because I had been a bad girl and had thrown up. I told Jim that I was not comfortable around him, and that looking at him was adding to my misery. I hated myself for causing him pain. All this fed into my *"I'm such an awful, bad, evil person"* belief. What was the matter with me? How could someone who is attractive, young, successful, and newly married do this to herself? Sure, we had problems with our marriage, but whose marriage is flawless? I have always tried to tell Jim that I cannot stop the anorexic/bulimic thoughts from entering my mind. It is not my fault that these awful thoughts and compulsive ideas are with me 24 hours per day. I did not choose this disease, and would not wish it on my enemies.

I have endured so much self-punishment, and so much self-abuse. Why?

It is sad and frightening to recall the pain I have inflicted on myself. It is almost as if I played Russian roulette with my life. How malnourished and debilitated did I have to get before I liked myself? How low could my weight get? How many times did I have to binge and purge until the urges left me alone? When would they stop hurting me? The answer is that they never will. And no matter how many times I binge and purge, the addictive drive to do so will remain inside of me.

I viewed the day after a relapse as a pampering day. I

had usually been throwing up for a couple of days straight, and my body was very weak. I allowed myself to get up and take the day off from my life. I could lounge around in bed and be lazy if I desired. I had special clothes that I liked to wear that day, ones that hung on my body a certain way. My salivary glands had not started swelling, so I was not dealing with the "uglies" yet. I was so hungry that when I finally ate, the food tasted wonderful. That was my Day 1, Lauren's Day. That was considered my pleasure time, even though I felt so ill. The more the cycle continued and the sicker I felt, the harder it was to get through that first day.

CHAPTER 20

LOSING MY LAST OUNCE OF DIGNITY

I feel as if I never really quite know when I have hit rock bottom. There have been so many bottoms that I thought were "it," yet it seems that when the next one comes, it is even worse.

Jim and I recently hit another bottom. It is something that I believe had to happen, despite how humiliating an experience it was for me. I need to share it with my readers, and hope that it does not change their opinion of me.

I was still lying to my husband and others about the severity of my binging and purging. I was buying large quantities of food to feed my addiction. If I could have thought rationally, I could have eliminated the middleman and flushed my money straight down the toilet. However, there is not one part of this disease that is rational. Anyway, the more food I ate, the more I wanted. In addition, the hungrier I was, the more I wanted to eat. The binge could consist of any kind of food, such as desserts, full dinners, or snack foods. During a binge, I could eat any food that I normally did not allow myself to eat. Judging by the number of grocery bags I returned home with, one might think I was feeding a family of eight.

The following is one of the most shameful acts I have

performed. I was ashamed of myself, and of how clever I had become with hiding the high grocery bills. I was using both my Visa and debit cards to pay for my food purchases. I alternated the cards, and threw away the receipts. I did whatever I could to get the food, acting like an addict going for a fix. I carefully planned each grocery trip and the excuse that I would use to cover it up.

My husband did not know about my food purchases. I lied about them to try to spare him the pain that I was suffering myself. I did not want him to be ashamed of me, too. I had to hide the fact that his wife was out of control. I would make up stories, telling him that I needed the money for a uniform or whatever else came to mind.

My last Visa bill was almost $300.00, all food. That was probably the third highest one in a row. I tried to justify the spending by saying, *"You earn most of the money anyway. This is your treat to yourself."* This was the only time that I let Lauren spend money on herself.

Strange as it sounds, this binging and purging was the one thing that I did for myself. I looked at it as my pleasure in life. When I entered the store, I did not have to worry about how many calories the food contained. I could buy whatever I wanted, and would immediately start eating in the car on the way home. I would hurriedly shove food in my mouth, gorging down as much as I wanted, vomit, and throw the trash into a dumpster to hide the evidence before Jim came home. It was complete abandonment of the binding anorexic schedules. I permitted myself to act recklessly. All the rules were broken, and I was free. I hated myself the entire time I was binging and purging, yet I could not stop. That must be the high I felt at the beginning of a binge. But about a quarter of the way through, I always realized that this behavior was not filling my need. It did not take the place of the pain or emptiness inside me, and I sunk to a lower level each time.

Late one night, after I went to bed, Jim took a look at the bill and receipts, and he knew the truth. He could have walked out at that time and have never come back. I would not have blamed him a bit. All the time that I was living this lie, I hated myself. The self-hatred intensified, and I despised the fact that I was lying to the man that I loved. Jim left me a note the next morning that said, *"We have to talk."* I had gotten up very early to go to work that day. I felt defeated and exposed, like a child caught with his hand in the cookie jar.

I had no excuse or explanation for my actions. I called Jim later that morning from work. I tried to be quiet, and allow him to express his anger and his thoughts. He completely surprised me and handled it much better than I thought he would. He said that he was not going to leave, but that I had to admit that I was out of control. I readily agreed. I tried not to cry, but it was futile, and the tears ran down my cheeks. Jim told me that he had already removed my credit and debit cards from my wallet. We mutually agreed that he would keep the cards and the checkbook. I would only take a small amount of money at a time from him to carry with me, and I would bring home every receipt from the grocery store. Jim said he felt like a tyrant and did not want to be in charge like this. But I told him that I loved him and needed his help. I had been asking God to change me, and to teach me how to be a more submissive and loving Christian wife. I wanted to stop being so rebellious, and stop acting like a child. This did not mean that I would let Jim hurt me or take advantage of me. It just meant that I needed to realize that I was out of control and needed the Lord's help.

Jim kept my cards for about three months, and this did help me to be more honest. I still slipped up once or twice. I did not have to confess to him, because he knew immediately. The power of these urges was still very strong and overwhelming. I was sick as a dog, sicker than I had ever been before. Yet somehow I could still find the energy to get up, scrounge up some money, and go to the store for food. I continued to binge and purge and work fulltime by constantly trying to block out the pain in my body.

I had two good weeks immediately after the credit card incident, during which I refrained from binging and purging. I allowed myself to eat balanced dinners, but was still obeying my strict schedules and rules. I still was not eating much during the day other than fruit, but at least I was not throwing up. Also, my body did not swell up quite as much as it normally did. At the end of these two weeks, I was craving the forbidden foods so badly that I ate them in large quantities and threw them up. Then the whole cycle started again, and the fighting between Jim and me returned. However, there was one big difference. This time I had lost my uninhabited freedom to buy food. There was always free food at work because family members brought in baked goods and treats for the staff in appreciation of our care for their loved ones. Almost any kind of food anyone gave me I would take, eat, and vomit. I secretively took any uneaten, leftover food from the patient trays to binge on. Food that remined in either the patient or employee refrigerators after a few days was mine. I justified this behavior by convincing myself that it would spoil and would only be thrown away. I even ate food I have removed from trash cans. How I hated myself and how disgusted and ashamed I felt. The guilt became unbearable. My skin color became ashen and pale, and I started losing my hair. I also lost muscle tone in my legs; to the extent that I could hardly pick my legs up to climb a step. The cramps in my shins were sharp and painful. The last time I vomited, I must have torn something in my throat, because I bled through my mouth and nose. To this day, my throat remains sensitive and sore. I also noticed that it was becoming much more difficult for me to make myself throw up. I hardly cared if I got all the food up or not. It took every ounce of energy I had to vomit and find the strength to crawl into bed so that I could sleep for a while. The dried vomit covered my face and my hair. If I felt strong enough, I would wash away the filthy evidence. I would then collapse on my bed and fall asleep.

CHAPTER 21

DOMESTIC VIOLENCE

I always felt that I deserved punishment, either self-inflicted or inflicted by others, because I had an eating disorder. I was a bad person. I just was not able to get past that feeling, that obstacle in the road that led to happiness. Jim had lived alone for many years, and had his own schedules and routines to which he adhered. He wanted to be the first one to look at the newspaper in the morning. He liked it neatly folded and crisp, and he read it in a certain order. One morning when he was in the shower, I had risen early and brought the paper inside. I saw an article that I really wanted to read, and began to unfold the paper. Jim heard me do this, and came running out of the bathroom. He grabbed the paper out of my hands and, in the process, accidentally twisted my arm. He started saying, *"What have I told you? This is my paper."* I was so shocked that I did not know what to do. I told him to let go of my arm, because he was hurting me, and he immediately did so. Later on, when he got to work, he called me and apologized. I knew that twisting my arm was accidental and unintentional. I forgave him and let it go.

The next incident took place about one year later. We had been arguing for almost an hour, and I had followed him back to the bedroom. He told me to leave him alone because he was very angry, and he had tried to shut the door. I sad *"no"* and just stood there, refusing to move. He moved me out of the way of the door, picking me up by the shoulders and throwing me down on the bed. My lip was accidentally cut, and that frightened me. I hardly bled at all, and felt very little pain. Jim stood in the doorway and would not let me leave the bedroom. He finally moved, and I ran out of the room, sobbing hysterically. After about ten minutes, he walked outside and sat on the lanai. When he came inside, he said that he could not believe what he had just done. He was extremely distraught and upset over his actions. I told him that I did not know if I could deal with

67

his actions, or even if I wanted to do so. It took time for us to work through this. I moved out of our home for about one week, mostly to show him that this could not keep happening or I would leave him permanently. I was responsible for myself and knew that I had to refuse to tolerate his behavior. I came to realize that we all come into relationships carrying baggage known as our past. I knew that Jim had some problems of his own with which he was dealing. These had nothing to do with me. I loved Jim more than I had ever loved any man, and I missed being with him.

I moved back home, and Jim tried very hard to change. About six months later the next incident occurred. It was shortly after Christmas, and Jim was still unemployed. I had entered into yet another bulimic relapse, and was rapidly losing weight. He became intolerant and unaccepting, and was furious with me for allowing the relapse to occur. Angry words were spoken, such as: *"How can you make yourself puke? Nobody's making you do this! I don't understand it at all."* He was very belittling and cruel. I believe this was due to his aggravation and frustration. He wanted to cure me, and had been trying to help me by listening more when I shared my suffering with him. But the relapse occurred despite his efforts, and he took it very personally. He interpreted it as my stabbing him in the back and intentionally hurting him.

We were arguing one morning, and he was saying *"Look at you, I can't believe that you're doing this."* He charged at me, grabbed me by the shoulders, and shoved me against the wall. He said that he could kill me for what I was doing to myself and to him. That scared me, and I again moved out of our home for one week.

Somehow, we got through that, too. Cliff and Darlene helped us financially by hiring Jim to paint the outside of their shop. Jim would stay with them for a couple of weeks, work, and come back home. He remained convinced that he had to move up there, and could not understand why I was reluctant to leave our area. I just did not feel that it was right, and I prayed and prayed about it, waiting for guidance from the Lord.

Our biggest problem was that Jim refused to acknowledge the incidents for what they were. He would say *"well, you upset me"* or *"this wasn't abuse."* It was too painful and humiliating for him to admit that he might have a problem.

We were unable to communicate with each other, and began to grow apart. Our mutual plans and dreams were dissolving before our eyes.

Another "almost" incident occurred when he returned from his last trip to his brother's. It started with a long and extremely verbally abusive phone conversation the day before, and grew from there. I had never heard him talk to me like that, and I was afraid. I felt that he hated me, despised me. I had absolutely no idea what to do, and I was trying desperately to pull myself out of a bad relapse. Through the advice of my Christian friends and counseling that I received, I decided to consult a divorce lawyer. I realized that our relationship could not go on like this. Things needed to change now.

I do not think that either Jim or I believed I would go so far as to consult a lawyer. I even canceled the first few appointments. I finally entered the attorney's office one day, crying hysterically because I was worried that Jim would find out that I was there. I had become afraid of him over this period of time, afraid of both mental and physical abuse. I almost walked out of the lawyer's office, but decided to stay. She was very nice, and she told me what my options were. We drew up some preliminary papers for a legal separation, and she told me to call her when I was ready to proceed. I said okay, and left her office feeling more hurt and confused than ever.

Meanwhile, Jim came back home from working with Cliff and we tried to move forward. I could not find the courage to tell him that I had consulted a lawyer. Despite our best efforts to reconcile, our relationship continued to deteriorate. I felt that, for my own safety and health, I had no other choice but to file for divorce. Coming to this decision was extremely difficult. However, my self-esteem and faith in the Lord increased beyond measure during this time. I consulted with ministers, friends, and counselors. Ironically, without Jim around, I was not binging and purging, even though I was living by myself. My physicians and friends helped me to realize that my health had never been as bad as it had been during the years that I had spent with my husband. I was harboring feelings of rejection and resentment, and knew that I had tried to change parts of Jim that I did not have any right to change. I looked at the whole picture, and I prayed very hard for direction and an answer from the Lord. At the beginning of my newfound faith in Jesus, Jim was not all that understanding. I think he felt threatened and left out of the spiritual changes that were happening inside of me. Jim believed in God, but after suffering through troubled times in his life, he was beginning to lose his confidence in Him.

I spoke with Jim's friends and family, to try to understand him better. When Jim was served the divorce papers, he realized I was serious about ending our marriage. He understood that I was able to go on with my life without him. We lived apart for a few weeks, and had many long and soul-searching talks during that time. Jim stayed with our friend Paul during our separation. God bless Paul. He has always been present when one or the other of us was in need. Jim and I dealt with numerous serious issues that were compromising our marriage. Jim promised me that he could deal with my eating disorder, and that he would learn more about it. He also agreed to enter marriage counseling with me, and vowed that he loved me with all his heart. And, most important, he vowed never again to give me a reason to fear him.

Jim was asking for another chance, and I was torn about what to do. I had always felt that Jim was the one for me. It was a very difficult decision to make, and I tried to stay strong and listen to my head and not my heart. We had owned our dog, Indy, for about six months. She became the child we could never have, and the three of us were a little family. Just as it took my buying a condo and asserting my independence for Jim to realize that he loved me, it took the reality of our impending divorce for Jim to realize that Indy and I were the most important things in his life. He knew that he had to start working at a steady job, and that we had to pull together to try to mend our marriage.

We had one marriage counseling session with a minister, and Jim even read a few of the Christian books that I had asked him to read about relationships. I did not know which books were right for us and which were not. I stumbled across a few at the thrift stores, and my minister gave me some others. Jim and I put all our efforts into saving our marriage.

Jim got a full-time job mowing lawns at a retirement community, and faithfully went to work every day. I realize that this was not easy for him to do, because he was only earning about one-third of the salary that he used to earn. I was proud of him, though, because he swallowed his pride and accepted this change. I enjoyed packing his lunch for him in the mornings, and sending him off to work with a kiss.

The biggest hurdle we had to clear was that I could not, and would not, live in fear of my husband. Jim started taking an herbal medicine for anger reduction. This was a big step for him, because he had always denied having any problems with anger. After he started taking the herb, I noticed that he was calmer. It always seemed to happen that the healthier I was, the calmer and happier he was. I can certainly understand this, and can even accept and understand his anger during my relapses. He becomes angry at the disease, not me, but he takes it out on me. Every time he looks at me, he sees the disease. Even my sister once grabbed me by the shoulders and shook me when she caught me throwing up in our parents' bathroom. I know it was not me she was shaking—it was the "beast". It must be very frustrating to want to help the person you love and yet not be able to do so.

I think back to the night I was Baker-acted to the psychiatric hospital. Jim came to see me, and found me sitting in a room all by myself nibbling on a graham cracker. We both cried and held one another tightly. He said that he would do anything to get me out of there. He said, *I don't want you to die"* and *Please, I'm walking around the house seeing your stethoscope and clothes, and thinking you might not come home. I can't live without you."* I believed him and could feel his love for me.

The last incident occurred a few months after we had bought our house, and during another anorexic-bulimic relapse. There had not been any more problems with abuse or fear until then. Jim had changed dramatically, having become much more understanding and supportive. I felt that I could tell him anything. If I was afraid to eat certain foods, I could share that with him. If I felt that my body was huge and distorted that day, I could also share that. We finally had a home that was ours. We really were very happy, and it was a good time for us. He was kind to me, and was becoming much closer to my parents. I was very thankful for those positive changes. He also started accepting my faith in God. He went to church with me once or twice, and did not belittle my spiritual growth.

Then the relapse hit. This one inflicted the deepest wounds in Jim because he really felt that this time, more than at any other time, he had done everything possible that he could do to keep me healthy. However, he had once again failed to keep me from throwing up. He was unable to keep me safe from the disease, and he was forced to watch me give into it once again.

With me, a binge and purge relapse is never a one-time event. The first time always leads into weeks, and usually months, of self-abuse. I have to become so crippled and weak that I can barely stand up, let alone walk, before I can even consider begining recovery. Once again, I had quit fighting my enemy, and raised the white flag.

I had hoped that I might succeed in pulling myself out of the relapse a little sooner this time, and was trying to make some positive changes in my behavior. I was more determined than ever to make two things happen, and I did: (1) I stopped weighing myself, and (2) I learned to eat a better variety of foods. I told myself that even if it killed me, I could not continue that scheduled eating. I had to force myself to eat better. I started by letting myself eat a good, balanced dinner. I still did not eat enough during the day, but that was always one of my biggest fears. I knew that I could not go back to my strict rules and monotonous eating habits. I prayed and prayed for the Lord to help me eat right, the way He wanted me to eat.

I had another binge and purge episode anyway, despite all the positive changes. I was disillusioned and losing hope, and knew I had to tell Jim about it. After I confessed, he refused to speak to me for about a day. When I tried to speak to him he was very angry, and his exact words to me were that I had *"shit all over him."* We had just finished painting our house and were both exhausted. On top of it all, he had not been feeling well. I am not trying to make excuses, but just want to paint the picture fairly and accurately.

I was standing across the room from him, in the kitchen, and he asked me if I had made myself sick that day. I said yes. He then asked me how many times I had vomited. I told him I did not know, maybe three or four. He perceived my tone of voice as flippant and cocky. Then, just like the other times with his anger, he got a certain look in his eyes. He ran across the room, grabbed me, and threw me down on the floor. This incident was the most severe and lasted about 20 minutes. He tried to choke me, and had me pinned to the ground. He hit me in the head and called me a "bitch" numerous times. I felt as if I was in a trance as I lay on the floor. I was too frightened to scream. I knew in my heart that Jim was not going to kill me because of the loose grip he had around my neck. I sensed that he was holding himself back, restraining himself. I did not feel that my life was in danger. I wanted to call the police, but I could not get away from him.

During the incident, I remember lying on the floor thinking that I deserved this treatment for putting him through such agony, and for punishing my body in a way that God did not want. Treat your body as a temple, the Bible says. And here I was abusing it.

After he realized what had happened, Jim began to sob hysterically, saying, *"I can't believe I did this to you. I love you so much. I can't believe I did this. I'm going to have to live with this for the rest of my life. I'm going to have to pay for this."*

I still believed in my husband. I did not think for a minute that he was capable of intentionally harming me. His actions just magnified the guilt I felt from the pain that my eating disorder had brought to my family. I live with that all the time, knowing that they are suffering, and hating myself for it.

The only visible marks I had were a couple of bruises on my hipbone and wrists. I did not mention this incident to anyone, and really tried to bury it in the back of my mind. I did not even confide in my minister. About two days later, I finally decided to tell my sister and parents. I was surprised that they did not seem very shocked or upset. I think it was because they loved Jim like a member of the family, and they saw the good that I saw in him. I have always defended him. I did not sound hysterical or traumatized when I spoke with them that day, either. My mother showed the most concern and worry. I had asked my family to be impartial and not to pass judgment on Jim, and they respected my wishes. I also asked them to be supportive and allow me to handle this myself.

The days went by, and I started feeling that Jim had gotten away with something. I was disappointed that he was not doing anything visible to me to prevent this from recurring. He still refused to go to counseling, and said that he would deal with this himself. When I mentioned that it was not the first time, he accused me of rubbing his nose in it and hurting him.

Towards the end of the week, co-workers saw the bruises on my wrists, and the nursing supervisor insisted that I watch a video on domestic violence. I found that our marriage had many of the characteristics of domestic violence. I learned from the video that Jim had committed a crime against me. I began to feel violated and exploited. After more thinking and praying, I decided to file a police report to protect myself. Social workers and other caring people convinced me that this was necessary. It was only paperwork, and it was time for me to stand up for myself. It was time to start looking out for Lauren.

With great reservation and nervousness, I drove to the police station and filed the police report. I also talked to a victim's advocate, who was a very kind and sympathetic woman. I was told that if I did not want to press charges against my husband, I did not have to. I chose not to. In the report, I wrote two pages describing what had happened during the incident. The first few lines were *"I love my husband dearly. He lives with my illness, which tears him apart and wears on him. I don't want a divorce. I just want us to get help."* Later that day, the station sent two policemen out to our house to talk with Jim and me. It was a very uncomfortable and unnerving situation because I had not told Jim that I had filed a report. He felt betrayed, and believed that I had turned against him. The policemen told him that he would go to jail the next time he physically hurt me. They talked to me about the women's shelter, and told me that I also had to take control over my health and psychological problems.

Jim did not forgive me for my betrayal. By the next morning, he was still unable to understand how I could have filed the report behind his back. He refused to go for any help. I believe that he felt horrible about what had happened, and I also believe that if he could have erased what had happened that night, he would have. Yet my fear of him was growing, and I was nervous and uncomfortable when he was at home with me.

Meanwhile, Jim's job at the cabinet shop was going well. He liked his employer and co-workers, and they liked him. He was rapidly learning the skills of the trade, and had not missed one day of work. About five days after I filed the report, the police came to the cabinet shop and arrested him for domestic violence. He was handcuffed in front of his co-workers and boss and transported to the county jail. The victim's advocate had told me that the pictures of my wrists and my story would go to the State, and that the State could supersede my wishes and press charges without my consent. However, I do not think the reality of this possibility had sunk in.

I continued to binge and purge heavily and was very ill. I was struggling to get through my day at work when I got the call telling me that my husband was on his way to jail. That was one of the worst phone calls of my life. My body began to tremble and my hands shook. I began to weep uncontrollably, and felt a hollow, sick feeling in the pit of my stomach. I swore to our friends that I did not press charges, and had not wanted him to be arrested. It was impossible for me to get Jim out of jail, since there was no bond for domestic violence. He was released on his own recognizance the next morning, after spending a sleepless, frightening night in jail. I had prayed all night for his safety and had not slept much myself. I was so worried about him. This was not what I had wanted at all. I just wanted him to admit that he had a problem and get help for it.

Jim stayed with Paul again, since he was ordered by the court to stay away from our home. He said he believed that I had not wanted him to be arrested. He said that this was, again, another wake up call for him. This was the shock he needed to change his outlook and actions. He promised me that things would be different, and that he would get some help.

Jim and I consulted a lawyer to learn our options. We petitioned the courts and were successful in placing Jim in a domestic violence/anger management program. It met for 29 weeks every Tuesday night and emphasized behavior retraining. We met the therapist in charge of the program together on a sunny Saturday afternoon. I remember that I held Jim's hand during this meeting. I wanted the therapist to know that I was supportive of Jim, that he was not a criminal, and that we had both been through a traumatic ordeal. We both needed help. I wanted Jim to admit that he had a problem and to do something about it. We had a comforting session with the therapist that day, and Jim attended every anger management class faithfully. I am very proud of him for that.

We also petitioned the courts to let Jim move back home and, after about two weeks of staying with Paul, he was allowed to do so. We were very cautious and reserved around each other, but tried to focus on that for which we could be thankful. We were trying to rebuild our lives.

Meanwhile, my health remained very poor, and resulted in a recurrence of thyroid problems. I would never make an excuse for domestic violence, and I do not regret involving law enforcement, because something had to be done. I had to take care of Lauren. I will say, though, that only until one lives with someone who is anorexic/bulimic, especially if he/she is one's spouse, can one understand the unbearable stress that comes from the aggravation, frustration, and continual setbacks. Jim has said that he can deal with this better now. It is very important for him to accept me at my existing weight. I believe that he will be able to do so. I think he is also learning that he cannot fix me. The therapist had told us Jim believed that when I was doing better, he was succeeding in fixing me. He loved me and wanted to make me happy. He always tried so hard, and never gave up.

I had to learn things too. I had to learn to leave him alone when he asked me. I had to learn to give him timeout times. I have seen such remarkable changes that God has made in each of us. My husband is now calmer, more understanding, and more accepting of me. I know that we both enjoy being married, and that we love each other deeply. We do not want to live without one another.

The realization that I could die from this disease is finally dawning on Jim, and it frightens him. I think it makes it worse that he helplessly watched his mother suffer and die from a terminal illness, and now he is watching the same play, with his wife in the leading role.

I have to be strong to not give in to this disease, and to never quit fighting. I have to keep winning more battles than I lose.

Jim's boss at the cabinet shop stood by him through the domestic violence ordeal. I chose to talk to him myself, to explain what had happened. Ironically, I felt like I needed to defend and protect Jim. I am so proud of Jim for continuing to get up and go to work every day. This helps me to feel loved and cared for. He has faced the humiliation he felt from being handcuffed in front of his co-workers.

We are both sorry for many of the things we have done. We have lived through many serious problems, yet have stayed together and grown closer. Jim is truly my other half.

Jim and I work ourselves into a vicious cycle. I binge and purge and have to confess this to him. He gets angry at me, and I feel guilty for what I have done to him. I punish myself for this by throwing up more. He becomes even angrier, and it keeps going and going. I hurt him, he hurts me, and I hurt myself. I feel awful for relapsing when he is trying so hard to support me. What is my problem? Shame on me! He has really tried with me. At one time, he even asked me to call him when the compulsive urges became severe, so that he could talk me through them. This, too, was unsuccessful. I hated myself for binging and purging when I hung up the phone.

After Jim was arrested, my sister came to Florida to stay with me. A very good thing resulted from that. Jim and my sister really grew closer as brother and sister. My sister came immediately at a time when Jim and I were both so distraught that we were at the edge of nervous breakdowns. We needed help, support, and love. I was extremely malnourished and underweight at this time. Cindy came and interceded on our behalf. At that time Jim needed someone to love him and be a friend, someone besides me. My sister fulfilled this role. She never judged him. She told him she believed that he loved me very much, and they got a chance to talk to one another honestly and openly. Jim truly appreciated her being here with us and could not thank her enough. Now, on the phone, he will tell her that he loves her, and it brings tears to my eyes.

Life is not perfect, but I definitely cherish the memories I have of happy moments like those.

CHAPTER 22

MY MOST CRITICAL RELAPSE

I became a born-again Christian. I was raised in the United Church of Christ and was always taught to believe in God, but I had stopped attending Sunday service. A few people whom I met through work tried to persuade me to give my life to Christ. I could not seem to let go of the tight reins of control and trust God to save me. After numerous, half-hearted attempts, I finally overcame my stubbornness and recited the Sinner's Prayer through a wonderful man whom I knew from work, Reverend Tony Cubello. He was in the process of starting a new church that would be named "Branch of Life Christian Fellowship." This came from the scripture that states that God truly is the vine and we are the branches. Tony was very down to earth, kind and patient with me. I gave my life to Christ and have never looked back.

I also chose to be re-baptized by Tony, and was submerged in the river near our home. This left me feeling cleansed, renewed, and rejuvenated. I could not wait to leave my old life behind and start my new one. Now that I was a Christian, I believed that my problems were all behind me. Surely the claws of the beast could no longer scratch and maim me. I was a child of God now!

Life ran smoothly for the next few months. Then thyroid abnormalities again recurred. Thyroid disease and anorexia—it became a question of which one would kill me first. They both can be fatal diseases, and one exacerbates, or worsens, the other. These illnesses bring out the worst in each other. I have always been the first to notice the change in my mental and physical abilities due to a thyroid imbalance. I know my body very well by now. My husband has become just as perceptive, if not more so, because of his emotional closeness to me. I began suspecting that my thyroid was unbalanced. I kept this thought to myself out of fear of being laughed at or ignored by the medical community. Many doctors have told me that my thyroid imbalance symptoms were only an anorexic/bulimic relapse. They also indicated that my problems were all psychological, and had nothing to do with my thyroid gland. I was also ridiculed by a few of them and treated as just another girl with mental problems.

I delayed asking for a blood test to check my thyroid because I believed I would not be taken seriously. I had fallen into a pretty bad binge and purge relapse, one that left me with severe nausea and head pain—sharp, stabbing, head pain that I had never had before. A headache from the binging and purging episodes is much like a dehydration headache, and is very debilitating. The pain starts at the top of my head, and radiates down to the base of my skull. But this was worse, and felt like extreme pressure inside my head. I felt that I could not take it anymore. I was unable to lift my head off the pillow without screaming in pain. I had dry heaves, retching uncontrollably until I collapsed on the floor. I knew that something was different and terribly wrong this time. My body was limp and crippled, and I had no energy whatsoever. It was all I could do to hold my toothbrush in my hand and brush my teeth. I had to stop flossing my teeth because my gums were raw and sore. I started becoming very depressed and bitter. I was angry, asking myself *"Now what have you done to yourself?"* I feared that I had abused my body too much, and wondered if I had it in me to rebound.

I finally gathered some courage and confided in my personal physician, Dr. Maggiano. He is the only one who never ridiculed me. He never promised that he could cure me, or acted as if he knew more than he actually did. He did not make fun of me or belittle me. Instead, he listened to me. We worked together professionally before I became his patient, and were casual friends. Maybe he does not know exactly how to treat my illnesses, and I certainly do not expect him to know everything, but I trust him and love him dearly. I know that he cares for me. He has never lied to me, told me something just because it was what I wanted to hear, or sugarcoated the illnesses. He has been a faithful and good doctor to me.

Dr. Maggiano ordered a blood test for my thyroid, and the results came back normal. I waited about two more weeks, and asked him if the test could be repeated. He ordered a CAT scan to try to find the reason for my excruciating headaches. CAT stands for Computerized Axial Tomography. This test would show my doctor a three-dimensional image of my brain. A tumor or internal bleeding could be detected. I tried to be a good patient during the test and follow the instructions of the technician. It was extremely difficult to lie still and endure the pain of my bones rubbing against the cold metal table. The temperature in the room was much too cold for me, and I tried to keep myself from shaking and shivering. When I sat up on the table, after the test was completed, I felt very dizzy and disoriented, and started to black out. The technician brought me a glass of orange juice, which I drank ravenously. My symptoms almost entirely disappeared, and I was able to drive myself home. The results of my scan came back negative for tumors or bleeds. My physician did say that I probably had cerebral atrophy, which is a wasting or decrease in the size of my brain, due to the years of malnutrition.

    I began to have difficulty walking. It was all I could do to continue working at my job. I used up all the vacation and sick time that I had accrued for the year. I blamed most of my suffering on myself, and began to doubt that my symptoms were from a thyroid imbalance. *"This is all your fault,"* I told myself. But the second thyroid blood test results came back, and my levels were extremely abnormal. I remember one level was supposed to be between 1 and 3, and mine was 53, meaning that my body was not absorbing my thyroid replacement medicine, Synthroid. Since I only have 10 percent of my thyroid gland left, I have to take Synthroid daily to survive. At this time, I was very hypothyroid, which explained my depression, lethargy, head pain and nausea. I was very ill but, believe it or not, the urges to eat and vomit were still there. They were the friends that never left me, the ones on which I could always depend. I wondered how I could possibly feel any more miserable. I just did not have the strength or the will to fight, and I surrendered to the urges. I figured that I was already suffering, so why not just resign myself.

    This was not the right attitude to take, but it was my reasoning at that time. So, I endured the worsening of both diseases, which set themselves to the destruction of my body. I learned that I was at high risk for meningitis, which is a swelling of the membranes of the spinal cord or brain. Because I had a very weakened immune system, my body was unable to fight off viruses and bacteria. My blood sugar was falling, causing me to pass out frequently. I was told that if my body did not start accepting the Synthroid soon, there was nothing that could be done to save my life. I went through a period of facing squarely my own mortality. I had thought about this before, but this time I considered it seriously. I had been in severe pain for so long that I actually wanted my life to end. I wanted the pain and torture to stop. *"God, please take me. Make it stop. This hurts too bad. I cannot function. I cannot do anything. Please!"*

Jim stayed as optimistic as he could during this time and tried to keep both of us going. He found it very hard to understand how I could still have urges to hurt myself when I was so sick. I kept telling him that this was the power of an eating disorder. He told me that he did not and never would understand.

Then I suffered my most serious, life-threatening event. It was 10:30 a.m., on a Sunday morning, and Jim had gone to the drug store to get one of my medicines. I was alone in the house, lying on the carpet with my head on the pillow that my dog used for her bed. She tried once or twice to regain her turf, then licked my face and curled up on the carpet next to me. I had been vomiting heavily over the past few days, and was very weak. I had gathered enough strength to walk to the bathroom, and was sitting on the toilet waiting to urinate. Suddenly, I felt the attack coming on. I became extremely nauseated and began to have violent dry heaves. There was nothing in my stomach to be brought up, yet the heaves and retching continued. My skin became cold and damp, and I started sweating profusely. I collapsed on the cold, tiled bathroom floor. The fall left me bruised and sore since I had no padding to protect me from the impact of the fall. My whole body stiffened and became rigid. My legs tensed up so hard and tight that for days after that, my calf and thigh muscles burned and ached. My fingers and toes curled inward and were paralyzed. I started calling out to the only person I knew that could help me, yelling, *"Help me, Jesus, help me, Lord."* My jaw dropped open, and the muscles around my mouth tightened and froze. I could not even understand my own words. I began to drool uncontrollably, and all I saw was darkness. I really thought that this was going to be the end. My heart was racing and skipping beats. I cannot find the words to emphasize the severity of the panic and fear that I felt. I flopped around on the hard floor like a dying fish, and did everything that I knew to try and save my life. I attempted in vain to stretch my arms and legs, and tried to keep myself moving. I did every little thing that I could but with no success. All I kept thinking was that Jim would come home and find his wife dead on the floor.

Gradually, ever so gradually the attack passed. My muscles relaxed, my heart rate slowed, and I was able to sit up. I grabbed onto the towel rack and pulled myself up off the floor. Clutching the counter top, I drank a whole glass of water, and splashed my face with cool water. After such an awful, frightening experience, I was surprised to be alive. I knew that only the Lord saved me from death.

One week prior to my attack, my mother and father had attended a medical seminar at their local hospital. They learned that my body could have rejected my Synthroid because I had been taking an anti-nausea medicine at the same time as the Synthroid. The label on the over-the-counter anti-nausea medicine bottle contained no warnings or precautions for use. I try to be careful and read every label on my medicine bottles. The medicine was a sweet, thick syrup that was supposed to relieve nausea, and I was probably drinking a bottle a day when the nausea was so severe. The directions were to sip on it every 15 minutes if needed, and that is what I did. Jim had suggested to me about a week prior to this that the syrup might be interfering with my prescription medicines, but I disagreed. I was convinced that I was dying from my own weakness and failure to conquer my eating disorder. However, I finally agreed to stop taking the syrup and see what would happen.

My weight had fallen to 70 pounds again. If my problems could be traced back to thyroid abnormalities, something that can be cared for and controlled, it would be a wonderful relief. People would sympathize with me and still love me, because that illness was not my fault. I just kept my prayers going and waited to see what would happen next.

It upsets me that many of the dangers of mixing over-the-counter medicine with prescription medicine can be unknown to patients. The pharmacist tries to be informative, but usually tells the patient to ask their doctor. I called the pharmacist, and was told that the anti-nausea syrup could most definitely interfere with Synthroid absorption in the body. I became very angry with myself for not getting prior approval from my physician. Just after I happened to mention it to my doctor, he ordered blood tests. The results proved that the syrup had been responsible for my previous abnormal results. My thyroid levels were slowly and steadily decreasing one week after I stopped taking the anti-nausea medicine.

Through the Internet, my sister found an article that described how the serotonin mechanisms of Prozac would not work effectively if the body was extremely underweight. A lightbulb went on in my head. I tried to use that as an encouragement for me to gain weight, knowing that my medicine would work better if I did so. I hate the fact that I cannot see myself the way other people do. I pray to the Lord to let me see an accurate body image, to help me look the way He wants me to look, and eat the way He wants me to eat.

I have noticed that even though I have not fully recovered from this relapse yet, I have not returned to my scheduled eating plans. I have asked God to take that from me, and He has. Remarkably, my nightmares rarely occur when I am eating well-balanced meals. I think it was the deprivation from only eating the same, safe foods that caused the nightmares. Time will tell. I still have some more experimenting to do.

Jim wants me to eat more throughout the day; he tries to help me. I keep trying to tell him how scared I am to take this step. I want to eat more and be normal for him. He cannot understand the complexity or strength of my fears. Somehow, I always relate being full and having a full stomach to being ugly, and that is not right. I want to stop thinking that way.

My body is currently going through the obligatory swelling phase. I am starting to puff out a little in my legs, and my swollen cheeks and glands once again give me the "chipmunk look." I know that this is a necessary part of the healing process, and that I must go through it. I think I am starting to deal with the swelling a little better, and Jim actually likes it. He says that my face looks less sunken. He likes it when I have swelling in my legs, because then they are more filled-out and look normal. He likes having something to grab onto.

I am still too sick to leave my home and fly out of town, although my sister has a plane ticket for me to use to visit her. My doctor said that I was not stable enough to go yet, and I am following his orders. My blood sugar was still too low. My headaches continue to be very painful, and are with me 24 hours a day. This frustrates and concerns me.

My doctor recently read me some articles on anorexia survival statistics during my last office visit. The mortality rate is rising and the success rate is declining—not very encouraging news. This is not the way I need to look at things, though. I need to keep fighting every day and take each day one at a time.

CHAPTER 23

FEELING LIKE JOB

During this time my weight dropped to 64 pounds. I continued to work fulltime. Just when I thought that my life could not get any worse, it did. A week before my three year anniversary at work, I was suddenly terminated with no warning. I felt stripped and naked again, and I wondered what else could possibly be taken from me.

Jim and I said that we felt like Job in the Bible. We had had everything taken from us. We desperately needed God to come in and completely take over.

I kept my faith in God. I continued praying to the Lord, whom I knew was taking care of me and doing what He had to do. I can now look at losing my job as something that had to happen, and the hurt feelings have decreased. I was hurt because I had always made my job such a big part of my life. At this job I had many friends and an excellent support system. I enjoyed the convenience of living three or four miles from my workplace. I loved working 12 hours shifts, and I earned a good salary. Jim and I were covered by my company health insurance plan. I realize that the Lord had to shake my life completely and do this, but it hurt when I was not able to see my friends. I felt betrayed and rejected by my bosses. I still miss all the residents, but I think I would cry too much if I visited them too soon.

The day I lost my job, I was at my critical 64-pound weight. That morning, I had finally agreed to let my doctor admit me to the hospital, put a feeding tube down me, start an IV, and administer the necessary medical treatments. I had agreed to give up the control and let them take over. I could not fight this battle alone. I had no choice. I had difficulty holding my head up, because it was throbbing so badly and my entire body ached. It was an effort to walk because my legs had no muscle tone left in them. My body had taken all the protein from the fat that it could, and now it was attacking my muscles, using the protein from them to keep me alive.

I made it very clear at the beginning of the discussion with my bosses that I was unable to think clearly due to my critical condition. I had tried to page my supervisor two hours prior to that to ask if I could leave early to check into the hospital, but she did not respond. They refused to delay my termination for even one day, which would have allowed my health insurance to continue to cover the hospitalization. I had to be terminated that day. I told them that I was in no shape to defend myself, physically or mentally. I begged and pleaded for my job as the tears rolled down my bony cheeks. If they had delayed termination just one more week, I would have received vacation and sick pay, along with other benefits that would have financially helped me. I received no severance pay, and my health insurance was discontinued. It was a very cruel experience and I thank God for helping me to forgive and move forward. I still miss my patients and my friends. It is not often that we find a job that we really love, and can look forward to getting up in the morning and going to work.

I called Jim to tell him that I had lost my job, and I drove myself home. Jim was very sympathetic and supportive. He has changed so much during our walk together through this life.

    Jim and I saw my doctor the next day. I asked him to go to the appointment with me. I wanted him in the room with us, to hear everything. I knew the report would not be good. My doctor, my friend, had already offered to treat me and get me through this critical stage, regardless of what I could afford. God bless him. He and his staff called me at home to check on me daily for the next few days. They knew that I had no insurance and could not afford to be admitted to the hospital. They began to involve Jim heavily in my care. That was the crucial part. Jim was included in all the treatment plans for me. He was with me in the examination room, and began learning what he could do to help me. He was responsible for weighing me daily at home, and calling in the weights to my doctor's office. I was to continue to take my medicine, increase my food intake, and, of course, stop throwing up.

    I realize that I can be rebellious. During the car ride home, Jim told me that he was embarrassed at how I acted in the doctor's office. My doctor wanted me to drink liquid supplements instead of eating solid food at the beginning, due to the poor condition of my stomach. I panicked at having what I could let myself eat taken from me. I felt that everything I loved and treasured had already been taken from me. I realized it was the control issue coming up again, and that I had to give it up. I just kept pleading to Jim and to my doctor, saying, *"Please, please, let me eat. I've been starving myself for so long. I'll eat chicken and vegetables for dinner. I'll eat a snack after dinner. I'll make myself eat more. Please believe me. Somehow I will. Please give me one more chance."* The thought of liquid supplements also brought back painful memories of when I had been forced to drink them during my first hospitalization. They represented sickness and failure. It is good for me to be able to eat and chew. I have learned that if I pick foods to eat like carrots and raw vegetables, I eat more slowly. Since I spend more time chewing, I feel like I can enjoy the food more and savor every bite. Otherwise, I fear that I would eat too fast and too much, be bloated, and end up vomiting.

I knew what I was doing when I had Jim come in the doctor's office. I was making it impossible for me to be deceitful by having him involved. I realize now that I had acted like a child during the appointment by whining and protesting. I understand that I need some "tough love" right now. I know that my husband and doctor must take a strong hand with me. I just want to say that I do not rebel because I am a brat. When I do rebel and fight against them, it is because of the great fears that I have. I want to be well more than anything, and do not want to die. Jim weighed me the next morning and called in my first weight. Team Traer was suited up and ready to face the enemy.

CHAPTER 24

SPIRITUAL HEALING AND PROGRESS

I still pray and believe in the Lord, and I know that he is healing me. I believe that He is teaching me things and changing me so that He can use me to speak to and help other people. I believe that God wants this book to be published. It is important that my story be told. Before I could be used by Him, I believe that the Lord had to break my spirit and show me how wrong I was. It was traumatic but necessary.

I know God is changing Jim and me. The other day, Jim told me that he said a prayer for me to get better. I started crying because it touched me so deeply. I have never known him to pray. He has been through so many ups and downs with me. My illness has affected his life directly through altering his moods and his attitudes. It affects what we can do together as a couple. We are not able to go out and enjoy ourselves when I am in a relapse, or in the first stages of recovery. My health is too poor, and my fears are too overwhelming. Jim has learned patience, and he has learned that there are parts of my eating disorder that I cannot control. He has also been my strongest supporter, and he continues to live through this illness with me.

Jim has done much for me. He has cooked for me, fixing me grilled cheese and soup when I could not eat anything else due to severe nausea. My stomach has gotten so bad within this past year or two that I have periods of nausea so debilitating that I cannot move. He calls to check on me from work, to make sure that I am okay. I smile and laugh as I watch him with our dog, Indy. We both love to roll around on the floor with her and play. She has really brought out the child in both of us, and I see how much Jim loves her. I believe that neither one of us was meant to have children, but we can shower Indy with love, and we do. Indy has always been there for Jim, to love him when I was unable to do so. She never let him down as I did. As bizarre as it may sound, I admire Indy for her eating habits. I fill her bowl with fresh food every morning, and she will eat little bits at a time, throughout the day, until it is gone. She never overeats, and knows when to stop. I think I could learn a great deal from my dog. She does not care what people think of her, nor does she waste her time worrying about things she cannot control. All she needs in life is to be fed, let outside when she has to go to the bathroom, and be played with. She loves Jim and me no matter what, even after we discipline her. She loves us unconditionally and does not hold a grudge. She trusts us to tend to her needs. It is the same way that God wants us to be towards Him. We are His children, and He will always take care of us. God knew we needed Indy, and He provided. He always does, and He always will.

As I have said, Jim is not physically attracted to me when I am so emaciated. I completely understand this, and try not to let it hurt me. He has to deal with the guilt that comes from knowing he is shunning me sexually because of how I look. He is becoming more accepting and understanding of how his rejection makes me feel. He has told me that he has always been the type to like women with some "meat on their bones," and that he would love it if I weighed 130 or 140 pounds. I really miss making love to my husband. It is something very special that only he and I share. He is the only man for me, and the only one that I want to be with.

Jim is also learning how powerful these urges are, and he is becoming much more understanding of my faith in God.

I do not know how my husband deals with the stress caused by my illness. He always tells me that when I am healthy, he is happy, and the difference in him when I am not in a relapse is remarkable. He is kind, gentle, and content.

I believe that we have brought out the worst in each other, but that we have also brought out the best. He keeps trying to understand, and needs to be able to separate me from the illness. If he wants to hate the illness, he can. But he should not hate me or blame me for the part that I cannot control. I must take responsibility for my actions when the urges come, but I cannot change the fact that I have this illness.. He finally realizes now that the scars are something we will live with for a very long time. He is insistent on regular thyroid tests, and is becoming more sensitive to my moods. He has matured greatly.

I have always tried to see the good through the bad. My mother is an eternal optimist. Sometimes she would be so optimistic I would want to say, *"Mom, stop that! This is not a happy time."* But that is how she survived the heart breaking ordeal that my parents have endured at the hands of my disease. They felt the sharp pain of watching their daughter choose the road that leads to self-destruction, torment, and death. They could do nothing more than stand by and watch as their daughter shriveled down to an emaciated replica of what she once was, and they watched their hard-earned money be flushed down the toilet, as she ate and vomited the food for which they had worked so hard.

One positive feature resulting from my illness is the relationship that I now have with my sister, Cindy. We share a very close bond. She stayed with me when Jim was in jail, when I finally admitted that I could not be left alone and needed her to help me. She was wonderful. She believes in God, and we prayed and sang praise songs together during her visit. She feels remorseful for all the years that she wasted being angry with me for being sick, instead of trying to understand. She saw my feelings and behavior as a choice, not as an illness. Within this past year, she has really tried to understand. These last few months have been such a joy. I would never choose to go through that pain again, but if it were necessary to bring us to where Cindy and I are right now, I would do it. She is beginning to understand me, and she comforts me. She was able to stroke my head when the headaches were sharp and severe and, for the first time, I was able to let her do that. My usual thinking would have been that the pain was my deserved punishment, and I would have said *"Don't touch me, don't get close to me, I've been bad. I'm dirty."* I had to learn to let her care for me. What a blessing that lesson has been in my life.

Even though Cindy lives in Maryland and I live in Florida, we try to talk once a day. My day just does not seem complete if Cindy and I do not have our early morning "coffee talks." We started becoming closer during times of tragedy for both of us. She had endured a failed relationship, which caused her heartache and pain. At the same time, I was in the process of filing for divorce from Jim. I had always viewed Cindy as the strong one, the one who held it all together. She was the aggressive and assertive one, the angry one, and the businesswoman who traveled the world. What a different side I now see. Our relationship has risen to a new level, and I love her with all my heart.

My parents are also still standing by me. My father is 84 and my mother is 76. They are slowing down, but they have never once given up on me. They have not stopped loving me or caring for me. I am thankful for the childhood I had. I do not hold anything against my mother for my inheritance of thyroid disease. I pray that she does not hold this against herself. They are kind, giving parents, and I love them very much.

This illness has given me a renewed sense of understanding and compassion for the patients for whom I cared. When they told me that they were in pain, sometimes it was the same kind of pain that I had experienced. I could genuinely say that I knew how they felt. They may have looked at me funny and not believed me, but I just told them,

"*Believe me, I've been very ill too, and I'm so sorry that you're hurting.*" My suffering gave me a larger amount of love and respect for them. I know what it is like to have my dignity stripped from me. I know what it is like to have tubes inserted into me because parts of my body had completely stopped functioning. I know the fear and frustration of losing my ability to urinate and move my bowels voluntarily and to be too weak to do the things I used to do.

I take nothing for granted anymore. Each day when the sun comes up and I am alive to see it, I thank God. Each day that my kidneys and bladder are working and I am able to urinate, I thank God. I still have yet to have my menstrual periods resume. They have been very sporadic these last 18 years, and I probably have not had one in the last three years. As my body weight increases, I believe they will return. I thank God for small miracles now. When Jim recently got a dollar an hour raise, I was just elated. I rejoice in the small things, and do not need much at all to make me happy.

I thank God for all the blessings in our lives every day. I fully believe that I have learned and matured more since I have been a born-again Christian than I have in my entire lifetime. I have grown as a person and have changed more than I ever did through all the conventional therapy that I have received. I have learned things through the Bible and through the Lord that no one ever taught me in therapy. I am still learning and have much farther to go in my journey, but I love and trust the Lord more every day. I also want His will to be done in my life, and I know for sure that everything happens because God planned it or allowed it to happen. Nothing that happens to me is going to catch God by surprise. Maybe there is a reason that I am still having relapses, and maybe there is also a reason that my condition has become graver. I used to think that I could make myself better, that I could beat this monstrous disease on my own. The cold, hard truth is I am not capable of this. Now I just ask God to help me by taking this controlling spirit away from me and teaching me how to eat. I want to be able to look in the mirror and be shocked and appalled by the skeletal image I see. I want to be able to look the way that He wants me to look. May He take these obsessive-compulsive and overpowering feelings and urges away from me. I am weak but He is strong.

I make a conscious effort every day to trust the Lord absolutely. That is much more difficult to do than to say, because it takes hard work, practice, and tears to let go of that control. He has answered my prayers and has healed my marriage. He is a kind and gracious God, and He has kept me alive all these years for a reason. Before I started this book I prayed for guidance, asking God if He really wanted me to write it. Am I capable? Is this idea silly? Would it be beneficial to others? Do You want me to do this, Lord?

I have wanted to write this book for a few years, but did not do so until I really felt that I could give all the praise and glory to God. I needed to do that first, and I needed to know that it was okay with Him for me to write this book.

I pray daily for patience and understanding. I thank God for all that Jim and I have been blessed with.. Even though money is tight, we have not missed a mortgage payment. We have dependable, nice cars to drive. We can afford to buy groceries and always have food on our table. We have grown much closer to one another as husband and wife, and our marriage has blossomed. I think of the people we were when we first met, and am thankful for how far we have come and for how much we have grown. Only God could have changed us. I can only pray that He keeps teaching me and changing me. Most of the knowledge I now have has been learned the hard way. I had to be tossed in the fire to have my impurities burned away. This is painful. I believe that God requires our involvement and hard work to achieve our own victories. By being involved we gain the knowledge that we are only victorious because we worked with God and not against Him.

I have no idea what my future may bring, but I know who brings the future. I thank God for all the periods of recovery when I was not throwing up or starving myself. Even if my eating habits were abnormal, I praise Him for the simple fact that I was not throwing up.

Now I have to work on my weight. I have been less

than 100 pounds for at least three years. There is still a part of me that clings to the security of a skeletal image. I know in my heart that I am less attractive when I am this thin, but my head does not acknowledge this. It is as if I am afraid to be normal, and afraid of how good my life can be. I have a husband who goes to work every day and who loves me. God has brought us through the traumatic times. So why am I unable to let myself enjoy this time of tranquility? Why am I holding back my own happiness? Most people would sit back and enjoy it, yet I rob myself of it. It just does not make sense.

Jim says he is learning that he cannot fix me, and that the disease is not my fault. I know that he loves me more than his own life, and if he could fight this "beast" for me, he would. Forgiveness is not an emotion, but a conscious decision that we make. We need to forgive one another, to love, and to let go. We need to stop beating each other over the head with the past. We need to get on with our lives and not look back.

I know that I am safe in the Lord's hands and that His will will be done in my life. I know that I must obey Him and listen to Him. I do not want to fail or disappoint Him. I also know that the Lord will take care of my marriage and my health. He promised that He would, and I know that He never breaks his promises.

I used to sit back and dwell on how much money and time I wasted on this disease. In my 20's, I never traveled, took vacations, or got out much. I was not a drinker, so I did not hang out at the bars. I never spent the money I had when I was single on enjoyable activities. I did not know how to be good to myself. I also try not to focus on the damage I have done to my body. This kind of negative thinking only causes me to hate myself, then abuse myself by throwing up as punishment for my past. There is no future in that.

I have to say that the closeness that I now feel with the Lord, the relationship that Jim and I have, and the relationship that my family and I have are of the utmost importance to me. I truly value my friends now, too.

I am learning not to worry, and to stop saying *"poor*

me." I refuse to sit around and feel sorry for myself when there are people who are suffering worse than me. Each of us has problems and suffers, and we are all just trying to get through them. For me, times of suffering make the good times and blessings that much more glorious.

I am still praying that God will take all of my anorexic rituals from me. Some of the rituals are no longer a part of my life. I used to look forward to that evening meal. I would try to make it last longer through the rituals of only letting myself eat left-handed, or touch, smell, and rearrange the food first—anything to extend the pleasure. Maybe there is a connection between delaying the pleasure of eating and delaying the pleasure of good health. Perhaps I feel that I do not deserve either one, and that these feelings would be too good for me. I have always had difficulty handling the good things in my life.

I want to be free, and I want to be well and enjoy my life. I want to be the best servant to God, and the best daughter, sister, and wife that I can be. I do not mean "best" as in perfection. I mean the most caring, loving, and generous person that I can be.

I have learned that perfection is not the measure of a person. I have learned that it is acceptable to get up in the morning and leave the bed unmade. If Jim needs the bed made that day, then he can and will do it himself. I have learned that life is not about perfection, and that we will never be perfect. That was a hard lesson for me to learn.

One thing that works very well for me is to keep my life as simple as possible and not take on too many things at once. This does not mean that I am stagnant or bored. Rather, it means slowing down and having a simple existence with my husband and my dog. It means not pushing myself. It means knowing when a situation is going to be uncomfortable, when it is a situation that I do not need to be in, and removing myself from it. I also know that I have to stand up to my fears because, if I do not, they will rule over me. I have to keep fighting, and I have to keep trying.

I have struggled so hard for the approval of others, yet failed to realize that I already had the most important approval I will ever need. It came from Jesus, who unconditionally loves me, and who died for me on a cross. If I had been the last person on this earth, He still would have died for me. How many of us would give our life for someone else? The Lord has always been there with His arms open, just waiting for me to turn to Him and let Him help and heal me. Nothing is impossible with Jesus. He wants us to be successful, happy, and healthy. He wants our lives to be abundant and blessed.

Little by little I am starting to feel better. I believe in my heart that my thyroid levels are still coming down towards normal limits. I believe that the Lord is healing me more every day.

I have a new goal. Statistics show that about 40 percent of anorexic women return to their normal weight. Twenty-five percent remain thin, but not thin enough to be a medical risk. I am part of the 24 percent now, and would like to be part of the 20 percent.

At this time, I am still unemployed. I love being a respiratory therapist, and there currently are not any open positions in the area where we live. The company I worked for has been laying off therapists all across the country. I live in an area that has an overabundance of therapists. It is a fairly small city, and we have both respiratory and nursing schools here. During the winter months, healthcare work is more plentiful, due to the influx of tourists. I have made numerous contacts, and am actively looking for work.

A glorious thing has happened during this time; Jim and I have become members of Branch of Life Christian Fellowship, Pastor Tony's church. We have about 25 members and value being a part of the church family. It is very comforting to be part of a family that cares so much about each other. They have all been praying for us, and have welcomed us with open arms. I firmly believe in the healing power of hands-on prayer. The first time I attended church, I was so weak that I had to be carried up the steps. I sat on a soft pillow, because it hurt too badly to sit directly on the chair. After one month, I was able to walk up the stairs by myself. I have since graduated from the pillow to the chair. Jim and I say a prayer of grace every night before dinner, and it is a dream come true for me. I had always hoped that he would pray and attend church with me. We had an incredible church service two days ago that was filled with the presence of the Holy Spirit. Pastor Tony anointed me with oil and the church members laid hands on me and prayed over me following the service. One couple has the gift of prophecy, and told me that it was not a coincidence that I had lost my job but that God had planned for it to happen. I was told that this book needs to come out and be read. Most importantly, they said that the demonic oppression had been lifted from me, and that God had set me free! I believe God spoke a powerful word to me and healed me that day. I used to feel like a demon had a stranglehold on me and would not let go. Suddenly I could feel the chains of bondage being broken off me. I could feel something wonderful happening to me. I had my fingers interlaced to pray, as I had been taught to do as a child in Sunday School. I felt the amazing power of God come over me, and every muscle in my body tensed. My hands were clenched so tightly together that I do not think I could have pried them open with a crowbar. I knew I had been set free. Not once did I feel fear during this glorious experience. I sobbed and sobbed as people prayed for me. I could not stop weeping. At that moment, I even wanted to start trying to eat more and was not afraid. For the first time in years, I really wanted to do this! I got down on my knees and thanked God for his healing power, mercy, and grace. He had given me a second chance.

Jim and I have grown much closer as husband and wife. Jim gets aggravated with me, and I get aggravated with him. Our relationship endures the good and bad times. We both agree that we have never been this close in our lives.

When we bought our home, the mortgage was based almost entirely on my salary. My salary was much higher, and now we are dependent on what Jim earns. I am extremely grateful to be receiving unemployment compensation while I look for a job. Filing for unemployment gave me a good dose of reality. It reminded me that I am certainly no better than anyone else, and that other people are going through hard times too. I need to think more about others and stop dwelling on my own problems. I am trying to face my fears and break the anorexic ties that bind me. I am making myself eat more during the day. I am gradually letting myself increase my food intake and am not beating myself up for it. To other people, it may not seem like the amount of food I am eating is a lot, but it is to me. I still only eat a grapefruit at noon, but have been successfully adding a bagel or popcorn later in the afternoon. Last night, I ate almost three whole packs of saltines before I went to sleep, and I had already eaten dinner! I was uncomfortably full but, instead of vomiting, I rolled myself into bed and fell asleep. I was so proud of myself!

I am praying that God molds and changes my body so that I can be healthy and serve Him well. I know that He has a great and wonderful plan for me, for all of us. I just know in my heart of hearts that He will not let Jim and me lose our home due to financial difficulty.

I have also been praying that God helps me to be happy for other people when their lives are wonderful and not feel jealous or sorry for myself because my life is not. He has already answered my prayer. There have been situations that have come up just recently since I lost my job where friends of mine were promoted, and I was able to be happy for them and with them. I need to be thankful for what I do have.

Over the years, my parents and my sister have taken many memorable vacations together. They used to invite me to go with them, but I have always said no, using the excuse that I had to work. Quite often this was the truth—I have always been a reliable employee who worked overtime and extra shifts. My career was the biggest part of my life then. But really, I declined their invitations because I was too afraid to come out of my cage. I was afraid that I would not be able to eat the special foods that I was comfortable with while away on vacation. What would I eat? How would I handle it? Would I be an embarrassment to them? I was so frightened of change, even when I was at a normal weight. I could not have gone on vacation with them and enjoyed myself. They journeyed to many nice places, including the Bahamas, and have memories together that I can never share. After choosing to stay behind, I would beat myself up, thinking that I was a bad daughter for not going with my family. I always wound up in a bulimic relapse while they were gone. It never failed that I would be binging and vomiting while they were out of town. What a waste.

I look back now at all the fun that I missed, all the family time together, because of my fears. I could not open up my cage and come out. The key was inside with me, under the lining of newspaper, yet I was unable to find it. I thought that I might be reprimanded for the foods I could not let myself eat, and not be accepted for who I was. I was afraid that I would embarrass myself by eating my special, safe foods in front of my family. Even if I was not throwing up, I was ashamed of my disease and ashamed of how I ate.

My family will soon be taking a two-week cruise to Alaska, and I want nothing more than for them to have a wonderful time. Jim and I were not included, only because I have always said *"no"* and have been so seriously ill. I am embarrassed to say that there is a small part of me right now saying that it is not fair. *"Why do they always get to go and have fun and I can't? Why do they get to do all the things in life that they've wanted to and I can't?"* However, the bigger part of me is marching onward down the road of recovery, even if I am only taking baby steps.

CHAPTER 25

HOW ANOREXIA AND BULIMIA DESTROY THE BODY

How does anorexia/bulimia affect the body? I am writing this book during and after my severest relapse. I believe this will enable me to describe accurately and thoroughly the pain and injuries that I have inflicted on my body.

I am going to be as honest and detailed as I can in this chapter. My goal is not to shock or offend, but to expose how crippling this disease can be. Perhaps other sufferers will have had similar experiences and, by reading this, will know that they are not alone and can also survive.

I have experienced three different episodes of lapsing into a catatonic state, characterized by stupor and extreme rigidity in my body. I had very minimal potassium left in my body. I experienced the symptoms of potassium deficiency, which are muscle weakness, dizziness, thirst, and mental confusion. My arms would bend up at the elbows and I could not straighten them out, no matter how hard I tried. My mouth would drop open, and I would start salivating. I was unable to close my mouth or speak. I was frightened that my heart would stop beating. During one such episode, I placed myself on oxygen. I believe that was what kept my heart beating. Unfortunately, this happened when my family was in Florida visiting me. Welcome to Florida, Mom and Dad! Here is your successful daughter! Are you proud of her? The look of terror and panic on their faces is permanently etched in my mind. How do I forgive myself for causing them such pain?

The second catatonic episode took place in the bedroom of our home, and it was my arms, face, and legs that grew numb and tense. My muscles were so tight and so sore that I was unable to move them.

The third and worst episode, which I discuss in Chapter twenty-two, occurred just a few months ago. I have great compassion and sympathy for people who suffer through life's critical health problems and literally cannot get to the phone to dial 911.

Due to the binging and forced vomiting, my throat becomes sore and raw, and a burning pain gnaws at my stomach. There is excruciating head pain. I cannot lift my head from the pillow without screaming out in agony. Dehydration, or the loss of fluid, results in severe muscle cramping, nausea, and lethargy. It also brings weakness, dizziness, and I frequently faint and collapse. I also endure constipation, low body temperature, chills, paranoia, and fear. The severity of the bulimia symptoms are dependent on the severity of the vomiting. I have vomited up blood, had a very irritated stomach, and experienced pressure in my ears and temporary deafness from the forced vomiting. There is severe pain in my sinuses, and episodes of near aspiration when I almost choke on my own vomit after a coughing spell. Depression, anger, and irritability are my best friends. I say vicious things and snap at those I love. There is self-doubt, poor self-esteem, feelings of being disgusted and ashamed of myself, feeling like a failure because I cannot stop this. What on earth is wrong with me that I have these feelings? Why can other people go out, eat normally, and be relaxed and happy? Why can I not do that without panicking, fretting, calculating, and usually throwing up after I eat? The *"why me?"* feelings are intense. And, I regret saying this, but I feel jealous of other people who do not have this disease.

Do I feel as if I am getting away with something, because I can eat all I want and get rid of it? Do I think I have the best of both worlds? The first few bites I take during a binge and purge episode taste wonderful, especially if I am voraciously hungry from not eating in many days. However, I am soon so weak that I can hardly lift the fork to my mouth, and then the self-hatred begins. I am extremely disappointed in myself, and I feel as if I have to start my recovery all over again, from square one.

It is not true that after a relapse, any progress I had made is null and void. No one can take my accomplishments from me, nor do I have to start from the very beginning. The steps I have taken towards recovery cannot be erased. I am still taking the steps, even if I take one step forward and two steps back.

I tried to change my eating habits and let go of some of the control during each recovery period. But fear and apprehension would overwhelm me, and I would have a relapse that was even worse than the one prior to it. However, I still made progress. I still continued to take the steps forward, and I kept trying. Each baby step I took was mental progress, and I could not let anyone take that away from me. I needed it to keep trying to survive. I had to stay motivated and think positively.

As I stated, constipation is a side effect of starvation. I still have problems with this. I have to use enemas to have a bowel movement. God answers prayers, and has given me a powerful sign of his love for me. In the past month, I have had two bowel movements on my own. After falling to my knees and thanking God for this miracle, I raced to the living room to share my exciting news with Jim. I keep telling him that I am one of a kind. I pray every morning, asking God to allow my bowels to move voluntarily. Oddly enough, when I first began taking Prozac, I had diarrhea. This is a common side effect of Prozac. The bizarre part is that when I had diarrhea, I felt happy. My body was cleansing itself, without my forcing it to do so. This gave me permission to eat a little more. I wish I could stop these feelings. Seeing them on paper helps me to realize how abnormal they are. Will I ever by normal?

Temporary kidney failure has forced me to swallow my pride and endure humiliation. I have had to go back to the hospital where I was the respiratory therapy clinical coordinator, see former co-workers, be severely underweight, and have a full bladder that required drainage with a catheter. I have been back to that hospital emergency room a few times for intravenous therapy also, to keep me alive with liquid potassium. With each visit, I had to reach way down and find the courage to show my face. But honesty is the best policy, and saying *"this is me, this is what I have wrong with me,"* and not hiding it is the best and only way.

I am somewhat pessimistic towards and skeptical about in-patient hospital programs, at least for me. I do not mean to dissuade anyone from seeking treatment. For some people, these programs may be wonderful and life-changing. For me, they did not seem to work. I do realize that I was very stubborn, always wanting to stop this destructive behavior myself, so that I could be proud of myself. I wanted to prove that I could take care of Lauren. I wanted to be given that chance, that opportunity to succeed.

I have also had horrible back pain that accompanied the kidney failure. I have had swellings around my genital area and armpits. My immune system weakens, and I am much more susceptible to colds and illnesses. I have extremely dry skin, and grow that fine layer of baby hair on my arms, face, and stomach, which is my body's way of insulating me and protecting me from the cold. I shiver constantly when my weight gets really low. I cannot think straight because my potassium is down and my electrolyte levels abnormal. I have to drink liquid potassium to keep me alive and keep my heart beating. As my levels stabilize, the liquid is replaced by potassium tablets, which I take orally. I have to endure many blood tests so that my doctor can monitor how efficiently or inefficiently my body is functioning. It is only by the grace of God that I have not fallen prey to the oral damage most men and women suffer from this illness. Most will have every tooth capped, many cavities, and even lose their teeth because of the gastric acid eroding the enamel covering their teeth. I have only had one cavity in my whole life, and it was before this illness started. My dentist and dental hygienist are amazed. They say that I have very strong teeth, but I know it is only because the Lord is protecting me.

I have experienced horrible leg cramps, especially in my shins, and pain so severe that I could not walk. Also, I have sores that do not heal on any part of my body, especially around my nose and mouth. I bruise easily. I have a large bruise on my tailbone right now, and I finally figured out that this is from the toilet seat rubbing against that bone. Jim had even replaced our old toilet seat with an extra soft one for me. My tailbone is swollen and sore, and has been very discolored for almost a month. The swelling does not hurt as badly as it looks. It is probably about two or three inches long and I know it will not fade until my body starts healing.

I have a hard time dealing with events of everyday life. I get irritable very fast. My moods are like a yo-yo, up and down constantly, despite my taking the Prozac. I get so mad at myself because I end up criticizing and insulting my family, whom I love dearly. Every little thing bothers me, and every molehill becomes a mountain.

I believe that some form of jealousy is experienced by most anorexics. When my anorexia was in its infancy, I wanted to be my daddy's little girl. I was jealous of my sister because she was four years older than me, and had a close relationship with my father. She did not seem to upset or aggravate him the way I did, and she always knew exactly what to say to make him smile. Being the older child, she did everything first. She was very intelligent and did well in school. I always felt that I was in her shadow. Recently, I came to find out that she spent many years being jealous of me for my looks. We wasted so much time misunderstanding one another.

I have hit curbs with my tires while driving because I could not pay attention to the road. By the grace of God, I have been able to work during times when I wondered how I could even get out of bed in the morning. I still tried to exercise by walking every day, sometimes having to stop and sit down on the side of the road to rest for a few minutes. I have been exercising in some form or other for about nine years, but it is one part of my life that has not become an out-of-control obsession. I take our dog for a nice long walk every morning before I go to work, even if it is 4:30 in the morning. But there are days when I cannot even do that, and have almost collapsed from severe abdominal pain and cramping.

It takes so long to sink to this level of debilitation with binging and purging. Whenever a relapse occurs, it takes about two months to get this seriously ill. When I do, I lose the desire to fight the compulsive urges. I can make it one day without vomiting, and will usually wake up the next day not cramping quite so badly. Tylenol will help my headache, and I can begin to feel human. Then, BAM! The urges come right back. Do it. Eat and throw up. Starve yourself. Give in.

The only thing that makes these compulsive urges subside is fighting it out, fighting through them. But once I start giving in, the urges gather strength and power. I have always had to get to a personal "rock bottom" before re-entering the war.

Every part of my body is sensitive, and hurts when it is touched. My fingernails chip and peel off. My eyes have bags under them. When I stop the vomiting, the swelling begins. It is extremely disheartening for me to watch my body swell up like a beach ball. My legs have been so edematous, or filled with tissue fluid, I could hardly lift them. My swollen skin jiggled when I walked. It usually takes a few weeks before the swelling in my glands is reduced and my normal body shape returns. I realize now that the swelling is a sign of healing, and I am more accepting of it.

Even resting on a soft mattress at night is painful, because my pelvic bones and spinal column rub against the mattress surface. I think what really hurts the most, however, is watching what the illness does to my marriage. I lack the energy to make love to my husband, and he is definitely not attracted to me when I am so emaciated. He has apologized to me for this, and said that he wishes he could feel attracted to me. He does not touch me, and gives me the impression he does not want to be near me when I am in a relapse. I want my husband to desire me. I want to make love to him. We are one body, as the Bible says, and when I hurt my body, I hurt our body. My body does not belong entirely to me anymore. Half of it belongs to my husband, as it says in the Scriptures.

I have nightmares of relapses and throwing up, even when I am in a period of recovery. Two or three months after a relapse, I have nightmares in which I am shoving food in my mouth and vomiting. I wake up in a cold sweat, thrashing about and screaming, because I am afraid that I have fallen off the wagon again. I think that I have finally made some sense of this issue. These nightmares were more prevalent when I was restricting myself through scheduled eating. I only ate certain things at certain times, which kept me from overeating and throwing up. It kept me stable and in recovery. In these nightmares, I was always eating the foods that I was depriving myself of in real life. When my diet is only tortilla shells and grapefruit, I begin to long for other foods. I want so desperately to go to lunch with friends and to participate in fun activities. This battle tears me apart inside. This also placed me in a lose/lose situation. If I declined an invitation to go out with a friend, I temporarily felt safe. I had protected myself from a tempting and scary event that could have led me into a relapse. But the self-destructive thoughts always followed, leading me to berate myself. These thoughts told me that I was running away from the issue instead of dealing with it face to face. They told me that if I could not handle these situations, that my recovery was a lie. How could I think that I was succeeding in getting better if I had to avoid things? Who was I kidding? I should be ashamed of myself. I was still a failure, and might as well give in to the urges. I was soon binging and vomiting and despising myself.

I also have very cold extremities. It is not uncommon for me to be soaking my feet in a bowl of hot water, four or five times a day just to warm them. I take a hot shower yet cannot feel the warmth. I have a constant chill. The cold penetrates my body with intensity. I can be sitting in the direct sunlight and still have chills. Some of the sensitivity to coldness comes from the thyroid disease, but most of it is from the anorexia and the severe weight loss. It is an icy coldness that pierces through me, even if I am wrapped tightly in a blanket.

I have wasted so much money on food and fluids. I always had to drink a lot of fluids during the binge, so that the food would come up easier. My husband used to say that at least with drinking alcohol or smoking cigarettes, he got immediate pleasure. All I was getting from my behavior was misery. Then, my sister helped me realize that there is something I get from this. It is a "high," a form of freedom that I feel because I can let go of my fear and eat everything I want, then vomit it up. It feels like liberation. There are no longer any rules or regulations on my eating. I am free! There are no self-imposed restrictions on when or what I eat, and no waiting to eat until a certain time of day. There is also a high I get from the starvation that comes afterwards, a hunger that brings a twisted sense of self-control and pride.

It is untrue that anorexia is purely a selfish child's disease that afflicts girls whose only desire is to get attention and be thin. It is not only girls, nor is it only thinness. It is really not even about food itself. The savage "beast" named anorexia can evolve into a horrible addiction, one that can have biological as well as psychological origin. I am living proof of that. It is true that I was focusing on my self and that my disease brought inexcusable pain and turmoil to my family. The goal I was trying to attain was to become so ill, so small, that I was dependent on my family to take care of me. Yet, I was rebelling against the authority of my parents by blatantly doing something that they disapproved of, something that would only hurt them. I wanted to show the world that I was growing up while clinging to the safety and love I had experienced in my childhood. I desperately needed an unattainable amount of love and attention, a need that no parents could ever fulfill, no matter how hard they tried.

I would give everything I have to get rid of this illness, even if it meant that I would only live five more years.

Malnutrition from anorexia makes my hair become very brittle and fall out when I brush it. My scalp itches and is sensitive to the touch. I get clammy, my heart beats erratically, and I have abnormal cardiac rhythms.

Since becoming a Christian, the psychological damage is much more difficult for me to handle. I value honesty, and I truly want to be what God wants me to be. When I am in a relapse, I lie, and the lies are compounded. I realize that I am lying, and hate myself for doing so. I have taken food that does not belong to me to eat and throw up, just to satisfy the urges. When I am under the influence of addiction, I do things that I would never otherwise do.

I also isolate myself, recoiling into my safe cocoon of disease. I want to avoid others because I feel so shameful and disgusting. Besides, how can I ever invite a friend over for lunch, then say, *"please excuse me while I throw up."* I never want to throw up in front of other people. It is a very private performance because it is a very disgusting act.

All things are free to me, as the Bible says, but not all things are good for me. One of the television preachers I watch has been preaching lately on the freedom of self-control. I seems like an oxymoron, but this is what I need. If I have no self-control, I have no self worth. When I am doing well, not caught in the binging and vomiting cycle, I feel like I can handle almost anything.

I am unable to make appropriate decisions during a time of relapse. I am very indecisive and unsure. Working in the nursing homes was easier for me because the pace was slower there than in the hospitals. I could never have been this sick while working in the hospital environment.

In the nursing homes, though, I could complete my assignments, even when I was working two jobs.

Alcoholics tell stories about how badly they felt the morning after drinking heavily, and that they did not know how they got into work. I always asked, *"How did they do that?"* Then I remember that I woke up feeling half dead on many mornings, hungry, and in pain, yet I made myself work 40-80 hour weeks. How did I do that? I do not have the answer, but I do know that it is now affecting me adversely.

My stomach gets raw and shrinks from self-starvation. The more weight I lose, the tinier it gets. When I start eating again, my stomach can only handle a small amount of food, and has to stretch and grow again with time. That is hard to tolerate. So is the nausea, dry mouth, and sores in my mouth from vomiting that take weeks to heal.

The illness drives a wedge between my husband and me. It also drives a wedge between the Lord and me. I do not even want to pray on the days that I am binging and purging. I am so ashamed. I am lying to my husband, wanting not only to be able to do it in a way that he will not catch me and try to stop me, but also wanting to protect him. If he does not know, or if he believes that I am just ill with the flu, he can accept that. Then, he is the sweetest most caring man in the world, and will do anything for me. If he knows that my suffering is self-induced, he has difficulty not getting angry about it. I cannot blame him, because I have wondered numerous times how I would feel if our roles were reversed, if it was his illness, and if I was watching him destroy himself. I do not know how I would watch my spouse slowly die, and not want to grab him, shake him and scream, *"stop, stop, stop,"* or tell him *"just don't do it, just say no!"*

One of my strictest anorexic rules is preventing myself from eating during the day. I can go all day, eating only a grapefruit, until dinner. I have had this ritual since the disorder began. I am very afraid of my stomach looking big after I eat. I ate close to nothing at lunchtime, and then, when I got home from work, dinnertime was My Special Time. Even if I just ate tortilla shells, I would allow myself to eat the entire pack. I was stuffed and my stomach was bloated, but that was acceptable. I did not have to go anywhere, and I could lie on the couch the rest of the evening. I really looked at that evening meal as my reward, my pleasure time. That was the only time that I permitted myself to eat a sizable amount of food. I am not comfortable eating three meals a day, or eating little bits at a time. I envy people who can get up and eat what they want throughout the day. I have not been able to do that since my childhood.

I just wish that I could be free, free from all the fears, rules, and regulations. Anorexics and bulimics must deal with their problems constantly. Jim sometimes tells me that I think too much about food and my fears. I ask him to remember that there are three meals in a day. Our society talks and thinks about food constantly. We have to eat food to live. Anorexics have to face and conquer their fears every day. Planning is involved with daily meals, even for "normal" people. Anorexics must convince themselves to eat the food, then learn when to stop to prevent overeating and vomiting. It is a battle that never stops. With dinner, I have to drink my milk very hot. Why? I make it super hot and then slowly sip it from a spoon, because I am afraid that I may otherwise drink to much milk at once and feel bloated. I have difficulty with moderation. I used to do the same thing with coffee. I still make cocoa so hot that is has burned the roof of my mouth and caused the skin to peel off. I am so afraid, though, of eating and drinking too fast, of feeling bloated, and of not knowing what my limit is.

I wish that I could see an accurate body image. I wish I could see what other people see, or how different I look. I can look at myself and at someone who weights 120 pounds, and the only difference that I will see is about 10 pounds. People who are overweight look fine to me. But for me to be overweight would not be acceptable.

How humiliating this illness can be. I think about all the things that I did to hide it, especially lying to Jim and myself about the money I was wasting on food. Sometimes I would eat large portions at fast food restaurants, then immediately throw up in the bathrooms. I frequented drive thru's, hurriedly ate the food in my car, and threw up on the side of the road. I packed two straws, a large drinking cup and a plastic bowl in my gym bag. I also packed one dry towel and one wet towel, to clean my face and hands. After buying the food to eat, I parked my car in the nearest secluded place, and set up a little table in my car. I proceeded to binge and purge until either the food was gone, or I was too weak and nauseated to continue. I threw up in abandoned parking lots, back streets, and dark places that were not safe for a single woman at night. I could easily have been raped or mugged. Throwing up on side streets became more difficult to conceal, but that did not stop me. Instead, I learned to double-bag garbage bags, eat in the car, throw up in the garbage bags and dump them in a dumpster. I hated myself for what I was leaving alongside the road—the vomit—how awful and disgusting. Could this be me? Was this really happening?

I remember hearing the sounds of disgust coming from strangers who had discovered my pile of vomit in the parking lot. I also recall the large, black birds who descended around my car to feast on my vomit. I always drove away as fast as I could and never looked back in the rearview mirror. On the way home, I would stop at a gas station that had a bathroom with an outside entrance. This was important because I could save myself from the embarrassment of facing the cashier, looking as awful as I did. I brushed my teeth, washed my face, and wet my hair. I also scrubbed my knees (they were dirty from my kneeling on the ground to vomit). When I returned home, I immediately scrubbed the inside of my car with hot water and detergent, again trying to erase what I had done. I still cringe when I drive past restaurants and gas station bathrooms that I frequented. These are the types of memories that create wounds that will never heal. No protective scabs form, because these wounds have been re-opened too many times.

I remember getting caught throwing up. I stopped at a fast-food restaurant, ordered the all-you-can-eat salad bar, and ate three large platefuls. I was vomiting in the bathroom when one of the workers came in and said, *"Excuse me, but if you have to do that, at least go outside by the dumpster, because I have to clean it up."* I was so humiliated. I started crying and saying how sorry I was. I was caught other times as well, in similar situations. How degrading and disgusting it was. But what I did not realize was that I was not disgusting. It was the illness that was the bad monster. I had to learn that I was good.

The only way that I could stop the vomiting was to eat the same food at the same time every day. When Jim would want to go out to dinner, I would panic. Oh, how I longed to go with him. But I could not let myself do it. If I did go, I would hide food in a napkin so that he would believe I ate and be proud of me. I would beat myself up all the way home asking, *"Why couldn't you eat that? You're so weak."*

I always wanted to be accepted, to be loved and thought of as beautiful. I think back now to all the boyfriends that I have had. During that time, I always wanted them to compliment me. I wanted to be successful so that I could be proud of myself, and so that other people would be proud of me. I wanted everybody to like me, to think that I was special and a good person. I was convinced that my thyroid and anorexia diseases made me a bad person. I believed that I was evil and being punished, because someone who was not evil would not do this to herself.

I still feel guilt, pain, and remorse for taking my husband and my family down this road with me. I have tried to forgive myself for this. I realize that it was all done unintentionally. I would never intentionally hurt anyone.

I have wasted many years trying to get approval from teachers and bosses, boyfriends, friends, and parents. But the hardest to get, and the one that I could never get, was my own approval of myself. It was not possible to meet my standards. I used to say that I could never be as demanding and cruel to anyone as I was to myself. I still believe that is true. One of the people that the Lord placed in my life a few years ago was a respiratory therapy supervisor who was a recovering alcoholic. She had been instructed by her sponsor to carry a baby picture of herself with her in her wallet every day. When she wanted to drink and harm herself, she was to look at that picture and say, *"Would I harm that little child?"* This is an effective technique. We would not think of harming someone who is innocent and vulnerable. We would never treat a child in the vicious and de-humanizing manner that we treat ourselves.

We anorexics and bulimics are not selfish, hateful people, nor are we evil. We are actually caring, loving people, but we just do not know how to love ourselves. We need love and yet we do not feel that we deserve it. We cannot accept the love that is given to us. We want so badly to be free, to be healed, and to lead healthy, happy lives.

I believe that obsessive/compulsive thoughts and low self-esteem are at the core of all addictions. These destructive thoughts continue against our will, driving us to commit an act that would normally be against our better judgment. We do know better than to do these things. We are aware that our thoughts are abnormal and try to resist these thoughts. We know that something is not right with us, and that we are different than other people. And, we despise this fact. We want to change, but feel so tired of trying and failing.

I think we should remember that all of us in this world experience pain, heartache, joy, happiness, and pleasure. We have successes, and we have failures. Not one of us is perfect or without our weaknesses. We all need one another to survive. We need to love, help, and accept one another.

EPILOGUE

I am now able to weigh myself. I see my doctor every few months so that he can monitor my weight. I no longer need to get on the scale backward to avoid looking down at the number. I am beginning to wear a bathing suit and swim in my pool. I know that my body is still healing, and that I have made significant progress. For some reason, I still get a certain amount of security from being underweight. Why?

One day at a time I fight my fights. I win more than I lose, and move forward more than backward. I am alive and growing stronger each day.

I continue to work on facing my fears and changing my

eating habits. I am teaching myself to eat more to grow into who I can become, and not fall back into who I used to be. I am still underweight and unable to see an accurate body image in the mirror. Why can I not see what other people see? Will I ever be able to do so? I do not want to see a distorted body image. I want to see what other people see when they look at me.

It has been over a year and a half since I last binged and purged or starved myself. Jim and I are both extremely proud of me. This is a very new experience for me. I used to think that I would have security and comfort by having a good job. But if I have God in my life, why am I looking for anything else? What more could I ever need? I know that the Lord is working powerfully through me, and I now have a changed Lauren and a changed husband.

My thyroid levels are now normal. Yet, painful headaches are a daily occurrence. I will not let them interrupt my life.

I will continue to faithfully take my multivitamin, Synthroid, and Prozac. I am slowly and steadily gaining weight. Some fears remain, but I am facing and confronting them. I know that I am being healed more every day, and that I have been set free from my bondage. I really think that God wanted me to work through this with Him. I believe that I had to suffer as much as I did so that I could be a powerful help to others. I do not think that I could be used to help someone else if I had not felt the hurt and pain myself.

It is not easy for me to be the receiver instead of the helper. I am a therapist, a caregiver by trade. It is what I do, and I find it difficult to sit back and let people help me.

Sometimes I feel that my remaining fears are an insult to the Lord, because I am showing Him that I do not trust Him enough. I do not want to be that way. He has changed me so gloriously already. I certainly do not want to be disrespectful.

I have climbed from 64 pounds to 100 pounds, and am still fighting this very personal war. I have always been a fighter, and always will be. I will continue to be a survivor, but I am only alive today and able to fight at all because of what the Lord has done in my life. He holds me and nurtures me. It is a miracle that I am alive.

The Lord always provides for His children. One week before my unemployment compensation was to run out, I was hired at Southwest Florida Regional Medical Center. I have never been so thankful and appreciative for a job in my life. I had been away from the hospital environment and critical care for five years, and was afraid that I had lost my skills. Thanks to my patient, highly skilled boss and co-workers, this past year at the hospital has been rewarding, educational, and enjoyable. I work 12-hour day shifts in a fast paced and unpredictable environment. The first few days were exhausting, and my legs ached by the time I got home. God has given me the strength and energy to work this job. I was even healthy enough to work extra shifts during the winter months. At first, Jim was worried and suspicious. In the past, I would work overtime after I had fallen into an anorexic-bulimic relapse. This was the only way that I could justify another failure to successfully fight the "beast" and win. The extra money I earned would pay for the food I would binge on. But, most importantly, my work was something that I could be proud of, and I could hate myself a little bit less. Besides, if I was working that hard, I deserved a reward, right?

I have successfully proved to Jim and to myself that I have moved past this old line of reasoning, and am capable of working extra and remaining in recovery. I used to believe that any sickness I developed in my body had to be my fault. I thought that I had to have done something to bring it upon myself. I am pleased to say that I have dealt with and overcome this obstacle twice. First, I developed a kidney infection and was placed on medicine that made me nauseated and caused me to involuntarily throw up. I *did not* force myself into a bulimic relapse, and was able to accept that this was not my fault! This was a huge success for me! Second, I developed an ulcer and irritation of my esophagus about one month ago, and had to have another endoscopic exam, (the first exam occurred at a time when I was too ashamed to admit my illness to my family, friends, and Jim.) I also came through this challenge without returning to self-punishment.

I took another monumental step forward by not relapsing during the holidays. I ate Thanksgiving dinner out with Jim and some of our close friends. I successfully ate a bigger meal during the day. I was extremely nervous and almost stayed home. Jim was very supportive. I ate the foods that I was comfortable with, and did not worry what the others thought of my food selection. Jim and I celebrated Christmas with Cliff and Darlene. Once again, I overcame my fears and ate a bigger meal during the day.

I am pleased to say that I finally visited the rehab center where I used to work. I still am unable to enter the building, but I stood outside and chatted with a few of my friends. I tried desperately to explain to them why I had not been back to see them. Both the buidling itself and my friends are painful reminders of a time of horrible bondage and oppression for me. I feel ashamed of who I was and of my actions. I thought everyone knew the severity and frequency of my binging and vomiting. I must have been a good actress though, and successful at hiding the evidence of my out-of-control addiction. I am proud of myself for taking this step, but do not think that I will return anytime soon. It is too painful and uncomfortable for me.

Jim found a new job eight months ago, but continues his search for an enjoyable career. I pray for the Lord's loving guidance in his life.

Jim occasionally gets frustrated when my weight plateaus, and he wants me to continue to gain. However, I know that he is very proud of me. He is my biggest fan.

I thank God every day for my marriage and for all the beautiful changes in it, for the undying love, and the strength. Having someone to share my life with and not suffering from loneliness really mean something to me. I thank God for that, and for keeping me alive for as long as He has. I know that He has special plans for me.

My husband is trying very hard to understand a disease that does not make sense. I love him for trying, and I would not trade my marriage for the world. I feel so close to Jim now, and I believe this closeness is helping me fight to live. I have to keep fighting to live. What I need to do is let go and let God finish His wonderful work in me.

I want to serve the Lord, and will proudly give my testimony to anyone who will listen.

With the love of my husband, the strength that I am getting from my marriage, and the healing power of Jesus Christ, I will survive.

GLOSSARY

Addiction. Physical or psychological, or both, dependence on a substance with use of increasing amounts. A compulsive need for and use of a substance.

Allergy. Exaggerated or abnormal reaction to substances or situations harmless to most people.

Anorexia. Loss of appetite

Anorexia Nervosa. Occurs most commonly in females between ages of 12 and 21, but may occur in older women and men. Characterized by intense fear of obesity, which continues despite weight loss. Feeling fat even when emaciated. Weight loss of 25 percent of original weight. Refusal to maintain body weight over a minimal normal weight for age and height. Malnutrition.

Binge. To go on an eating spree, overeating, stuffing oneself.

Bulimia. Excessive and insatiable appetite. A neurotic disorder especially of young adolescents and younger women characterized by bouts of overeating followed by voluntary vomiting, fasting, or induced diarrhea. An abnormal and constant craving for food. A serious eating disorder chiefly in females.

Compulsion. Repetitive act performed to relieve fear connected with obsession; dictated by the patient's subconscious against the patient's wishes and, if denied, causing uneasiness.

Compulsive idea. An idea that continues against one's will to suggest the commitment of an overt act that would normally be against one's better judgement.

Depression. A psychological disorder marked by: sadness, inactivity, difficulty in thinking and concentration, and feelings of dejection, altered mood swings, poor appetite, lack of or excessive sleeping, decreased sex drive, loss of energy, feelings of worthlessness and excessive guilt, recurrent thought of death and/or suicide.

Disease. An abnormal bodily condition that impairs functioning and can usually be recognized by signs and symptoms: sickness.

Diuretic. An agent that increases the secretion of urine.

Emaciate. To become or cause to become very thin; malnutrition.

Exacerbate. To make more violent, bitter, or severe. Increase in the severity of a disease.

Goiter. An enlargement of the thyroid gland. May be due to lack of iodine in diet, thyroiditis, inflammation from infection, tumors, or hyper or hypofunction of the thyroid gland.

Graves Disease. Also called exopthmalmic goiter, hyperthyroidism. Symptoms: bulging eyeballs, enlarged thyroid, tremor of fingers, increased heart rate, increased metabolism, vomiting and diarrhea, profuse perspiration, nervous irritability, skin eruptions, emaciation, anemia, and hyperglycemia.

Iodine. A nonmetallic chemical element used especially in medicine and photography. Aids in the development and functioning of the thyroid gland, formation of thyroxin, and prevention of goiter.

Laxative. Relieving constipation. A food or chemical substance that acts to loosen the bowels.

Metabolism. The processes by which a substance is broken down and used in the body.

Obsession. The neurotic mental state of having an uncontrollable desire to dwell on an idea or an emotion. The patient is aware of the abnormality and resists these thoughts.

Obsessive-Compulsion. An inclination to perform certain rituals repetitiously in order to relieve anxiety.

Propylthiouracil (PTU). A thyroid hormone antagonist that inhibits thyroid hormone formation.

Prozac (Fluoxetine Hydrochloride). Anti-depressant and antiobsessive/compulsive medicine for oral administration. Inhibits reuptake of serotonin by the central nervous system.

Purge. To cleanse or purify, especially from sin. To cause strong and repeated emptying of the bowels.

Radioactive Iodine. An isotope of iodine used in diagnosis of thyroid disorders. Used in the treatment of toxic goiter and thyroid carcinoma by destroying thyroid tissues.

Radium. A very radioactive metallic chemical element used in the treatment of cancer.

Recovery. The process of becoming well and returning to a state of health. To regain normal health, poise, or status. To make up for, reclaim.

Regurgitate. To throw, or be thrown back up or out, as with food.

Relapse. To slip or fall back into a former worse state (as of illness). A recurrence of illness after a period of improvement.

Registered Respiratory Therapist (RRT). Credentials

given to an individual who successfully passes the advanced practitioner levels of an examination given by the National Board of Respiratory Care.

Respiratory Therapist. Person who by training and background is qualified to provide respiratory therapy.

Respiratory Therapy. Treatment to preserve or improve lung function. A profession that studies and treats patients with pulmonary disease.

Serotonin. A neurotransmitter thought to be involved in neural mechanisms important in sleep and sensory perception.

Synthroid (Levothyroxine Sodium). A thyroid hormone given by mouth in an attempt to regulate thyroid function, verified by prescribed blood testing.

Thyroid. A gland of internal secretion in the base of the neck, anterior and partially surrounding the thyroid cartilage and upper rings of the trachea. The thyroid gland is enlarged in goiter and may pulosate.

Trachea. Windpipe. The main tube by which air enters the lung of vertebrates.

Tracheotomy. Incision of the trachea through the skin and muscles of the neck overlying the trachea.

Vomit. To throw up or expel the contents of the stomach through the mouth.

MEDICAL CONSEQUENCES OF EATING DISORDERS

ANOREXIA NERVOSA

Heart Problems: Starvation can result in the heart muscle shrinking, slowing down and beating irregularly. The potential for heart failure must be taken seriously. Cardiac arrhythmia is often found in anorectics and can be a cause of sudden death.

Amenorrhea: The cessation of menstruation occurs frequently in anorectic patients, often before extensive weight loss occurs.

Kidneys: Anorectic behavior can lead to dehydration, kidney stones and kidney failure.

Lanugo: A fine body hair can develop on the bodies of anorectics. It is often seen on the arms and can even cover the person's face.

Muscle Atrophy: Significant weight loss often leads to deterioration of muscle tissue.

Digestive Problems: Restricted eating can result in delayed gastric emptying, making bowel irritation and constipation a problem.

Osteoporosis: Can develop during anorexia nervosa or later in life, even after eating has normalized for years.

Anemia, Altered Brain Function & Size and Reduced Body Temperature

BULIMIA NERVOSA

Electrolyte Imbalance: Vomiting and the use of laxatives and diuretics can cause sodium and potassium to be flushed out of the body. This can cause heart arrhythmia, heart failure and death.

Dental Problems: The stomach acids in vomit erode teeth enamel, leading to extensive cavities and damage. Gum erosion is also common.

Throat/esophagus/stomach: Self-induced vomiting can result in irritation and tears in the lining of the throat, esophagus and stomach.

Laxative Dependence: Abusing laxatives can result in the inability to have normal bowel movements.

Emetic Toxicity: Abuse of emetics such as Syrup of Ipecac, can lead to toxicity, heart failure and death.

Swollen Glands: Vomit irritates and results in the swelling of the glands around the neck and face.

Muscular Weakness (including the heart), Edema, Vitamin Deficiencies, Central Nervous System Disturbances.

(NOTE: Bulimics who are unsuccessful in weight-control are also subject to all of the problems of compulsive overeaters.)

COMPULSIVE OVEREATING/OVERWEIGHT

High Blood Pressure: Excess weight is believed to be a cause of hypertension in many individuals.

High Cholesterol Levels: Compulsive eating, especially on foods high in sugar or fat content, leads to elevated cholesterol levels and hardening of the arteries.

Heart Disease: Excess weight taxes the heart muscle, causes high blood pressure, hardening of the arteries and elevated cholesterol and triglyceride levels, all of which are associated with heart disease, including heart attacks.

Diabetes: Excess weight is associated with an increased risk of diabetes. Overeating simple carbohydrates, including sweets and junk food, places stress on the pancreas, which can lead to reactive hypoglycemia early in life and secondary diabetes later because of increase insulin resistance.

Reference: The Willough Healthcare System, Naples, Florida

BIBLIOGRAPHY

1. Burton G., Hodgkin E., Ward J.: Respiratory Care: A Guide to Clinical Practice, ed. 4. Philadelphia: Lippincott-Raven Publishers, 1984

2. Thomas, Clayton L.: Taber's Cyclopedic Medical Dictionary, ed. 15. Philadelphia, 1985. F.A. Davis Company, 1985

3. Physician's Desk Reference, ed. 51. Montvale: Medical Economics company, Inc. 1997.

4. The Everyday Study Bible, New Century Version. Dallas: Word Publishing, 1991

TESTIMONIALS

When Lauren Traer first came to my office for medical help, she was in denial regarding her illness. She was suffering with weight loss, physical symptoms, depression, anxiety and fatigue. After intensive evaluation, Lauren was diagnosed with an eating disorder. Her individual treatment involved trial and error and included medication, medical and psychological therapy, and nutritional support and guidance.

Unfortunately, at this time there are no quick or easy answers or cures to an eating disorder. Over time, she has reached an understanding of this disease. She realizes that eating and weight gain (or loss) is her responsibility. Lauren has discovered new ways of "nourishing" herself with food that strengthens her inner resources and sustains her.

I am very proud of Lauren. She continually faces a day to day battle in order to remain healthy. Every day she combats this disease and now is sharing her story in order to help others through the same struggle and survival.

Robert B. Maggiano, D.O., A.B.F.P.

"An inspiration to those who suffer daily from this disease. Lauren has given a very sincere portrayal of her struggle to cope with such a devastating illness."

Ashley Larier, BSN, RN

"Lauren is truly a remarkable example of the power of the living God. When I first met her, she wasn't expected to live. Today, she is a vibrant testimony to the healing and love of Jesus! This book brings hope and strength to the many who suffer in silence and is a must read."

"Lauren and Jim Traer are a blessing to our congregation. They have defeated, through the power of God, the grip of a disease that is seldom discussed in today's society. Through prayer and self-determination, Lauren continues to overcome and is a living witness to the healing and strength of Jesus Christ in her life."

When Lauren Traer first came to me, there was hopelessness and despair in her spirit that was beyond understanding. Suffering silently with this destructive disease, she was on the

very edge of death. Through the mercy of God, the power of prayer and her shear determination, she has come back from death's door to share her experiences and love for Jesus, with others who share in her struggle to be free from this silent killer."
>
> Rev. Anthony Cubello, III, Senior Pastor
> The Branch of Life Christian Fellowship
> Cape Coral, Florida

"This book is not only an autobiography; it is a narrative of the tragedies and triumphs of a person wrestling with a life-threatening compulsion. The reader will discover the book to be both informative and moving."
>
> Mark A. Ehman, Ph.D.

"Domestic violence is based on power and control. A parent-child relationship is based on power and control from birth to eighteen. A spouse relationship is not based on power and control. When one spouse has a problem and does not do anything to take care of their problem, the health spouse starts to become controlling to help the spouse with the problem. Jim became the parent and Lauren was the child. Jim became controlling in order to make her well. The domestic violence issues had to be addressed separately from Lauren's problems. Lauren and Jim demonstrate that both parties have to change and take responsibility for themselves to endure time. The recovery process made Jim and Lauren realize that they could not control each other. The reunification came quickly with rules for each party to follow. There have been no more incidents of domestic violence."
>
> Bill Bohs, M.A.
> Licensed Mental Health Counselor
> Certified Addiction Professional
> Certified Family Mediator

"This is a story that needs to be told and needs to be shared. A story of desperation, depression and anguish that finally leads to triumph. This is a real modern-day 'miracle'."
>
> Jeanne Henshaw, R.N.

I had the privilege of working with Lauren at a rehabilitation center where I'm employed as an R.N. When I first met her, almost three years ago, I noted a very pretty, young lady with a winsome smile. It was only when I put my arms around her to give her a hug, that I realized there was a real problem. We were sharing our faith at the time. Loren had just become a Christian and I was overcome with joy at finding another that shared my faith in Jesus. That hug made me realize that she was fighting for her life and that she couldn't do it alone. I prayed silently that the Lord would give Lauren the strength to overcome her eating disorder and all the underlying depression that causes a person to become anorexic and bulimic.

I watched Lauren walk away and my heart cried for her. She wore clothes miles too large. They just hung on a frame that was little more than a skeleton covered with skin. I remembered, as a teen, seeing someone that thin and who died shortly after. I knew Lauren's fate and prayed that God would give her super human strength to overcome this addiction.

Lauren was invited to attend Branch of Life Christian Fellowship. She arrived that day in an extremely weakened condition, and attempted to climb the outside stairs that lead to our small church, but was unable to make it. She had no strength. Her body was ravaged to a mere 64 pounds. John, my husband, scooped her up in his arms and carried her up the flight of stairs. He said it was like picking up a feather, she was so light.

At the end of the service, we prayed for Lauren and asked God to intervene. We knew she was dying and believed that the strength Lauren needed to regain her health would take a real miracle.

A few weeks later, at the Rehab Center, Lauren came up to me and said that she no longer had a job; they were cutting down on respiratory therapists, and no longer needed her. I know this was a real blow because I had had a similar experience. I knew Lauren loved what she was doing and her patient's loved her. In spite of inner turmoil, she always had a smile, a warm touch and a caring, compassionate nature. I could sense that she felt this was totally unfair and, in part, due to the health problems she was having with her anorexia. Just when she was at her lowest, she was delivered another blow.

Thank God for her new found faith, a caring, supportive husband and Christian friends that spurred her on with love, encouragement and prayer.

A few weeks later, Lauren signed up to pack food for a local food bank. We all noticed a fantastic change in Lauren's body and strength. She could carry two heavy bags of sorted food clear across the room, which she did several times. She literally ran across the parking lot with bounce in her step and a vigor that was not there before. It was during this time that she was accepted for a R.T. position at a local hospital.

God was enabling Lauren to regain her health, her self-esteem and literally giving her life. It has been a slow healing process, a healing of mind and body. It has been a day to day walk with strength far greater than human strength.

I look at Lauren now and my faith is bolstered. Many say they have never seen a miracle. I can say the Lauren's life is definitely a miracle.

Because she has lived this book, it is my hope and prayer that others, like her, will have a greater understanding of anorexia and bulimia. Only when you have gone through, and have overcome a problem or crisis, can you possible reach out or even understand another's plight.

May this book enlighten, touch, and heal lives.

God bless you Lauren. Keep reaching for the stars!

Jeanne Henshaw, R.N.